★

THE TWILIGHT OF THE PRESIDENCY

George E.
Reedy

New York and Cleveland

The twi-light of the pres-idency

An NAL *Book*
The World Publishing Company

★

This book is dedicated to my father for reasons that he would have understood perfectly.

Contents

	FOREWORD	xi
I	THE AMERICAN MONARCHY	3
II	THE BURDEN OF SISYPHUS	18
III	THE PRESIDENTIAL GAMBIT	33
IV	THE MONOPOLY OF AUTHORITATIVE ANSWERS	48
V	POLITICAL INFLEXIBILITY	61
VI	CABINET AND CONGRESS	73
VII	THE PRESSURE COOKER	85
VIII	THE PRESIDENCY AND THE PRESS	99
IX	THE FIFTH WHEEL	119
X	TO TINKER WITH THE MACHINERY	136
XI	THE WIDENING GAP	155
XII	IT CAN HAPPEN	168
XIII	THE LENGTHENING SHADOWS	181
	CONCLUSION	195
	INDEX	199

★

Foreword

The most frequently asked question of any former presidential assistant is whether he misses the White House. My answer is a heartfelt no!

It is an institution which can be regarded with a far higher degree of approbation from the outside—where reverence softens the harsh lines of reality—than from the inside. Like any impressionistic painting, it improves with distance.

My instinctive reactions to the White House have undoubtedly colored this book, although I have tried to eliminate personalities as much as possible. This is not a scholarly work, much as I respect scholarship, simply because I am not a scholar and am not seeking to invade a domain where I have no credentials. It is not based upon exhaustive research even though I have read most of the standard works on the presidency, many of which are excellent. Basically, this is an attempt to explain to myself and others what I have seen and what has been done in terms of my general knowledge of American and world history.

This does not mean that I am suggesting scholars should ignore this book. Quite the contrary. I am hoping they will take it into account in their researches. If it indicates some new directions, it will have accomplished a purpose. And the one thing that is clear at the time of this writing is that some new directions are indicated if our society is to survive.

The factor that I have missed in most of the works on the presidency I have read is the impact of the institution on individuals. The literature on the subject seems to assume that the White House somehow molds the man and his assistants into finer forms and that the major problem of government is to assure channels through which these forms will have full expression. It is virtually taken for granted that the proper objective of a study of our chief executive is to identify those inhibiting factors which frustrate his efforts to resolve national problems and to devise mechanisms which will remove those frustrations. This is a type of study which should be continued on a priority basis. The frustrations are many and could be catastrophic.

But the analysis is inadequate. It ignores the fundamental reality of society, which is that institutions are manned by individual human beings and that government —regardless of the managerial flow charts produced by the behavioral scientists—is still a question of decisions that are made by people. The basic question is not whether we have devised structures with inadequate authority for the decision-making process. The question is whether the structures have created an environment in which men cannot function in any kind of a decent and humane relationship to the people whom they are supposed to lead. I am afraid—and on this point I am a pessimist—that we have devised that kind of a system.

To explain this, I must start with a highly personal reaction. The trouble with the White House—for anyone who is a part of it—is that when he picks up a telephone and tells people to do something, they usually do it. They may sabotage the project, after they have hung up the phone. They may stall, hoping that "the old son of a bitch" will forget about it. They may respond with an avalanche of statistics and briefing papers in which the original purpose will be lost and life will continue as before. But the heel click at the other end of the wire will be audible and the response—however invalid—will be prompt. There will be no delay in assurance, however protracted may be performance.

This is an unhealthy environment for men and women whose essential business is to deal with people in large numbers. It is soothing to the ego, but it fosters illusions about humanity. It comforts the weary assistant who may have gone round the clock in his search for a solution to an insoluble problem, but it paves the way for massive disillusionment. And for the very young, the process is demoralizing. It creates a picture of the world which is ill adapted to that which they will face once the days of glory come to an end. There should be a flat rule that no one be permitted to enter the gates of the White House until he is at least forty and has suffered major disappointments in life.

My own heart is back in the Senate, where I spent so many years of my adult life either as a newspaperman or a staff assistant. This is not because the people at the other end of Pennsylvania Avenue are any better in terms of character, wisdom, or goals. It is simply that their egos must face daily clashes with similarly strong egos who stand on a par and who do not feel any sense of subordination. In the Senate, no course stands the remotest chance of adoption unless a minimum of fifty-one egotistical men

are persuaded of its wisdom, and in some cases the minimum is sixty-seven. These are preconditions under which
even the most neurotic of personalities must make some
obeisance to reality.

The inner life of the White House is essentially the life
of the barnyard, as set forth so graphically in the study
of the pecking order among chickens which every freshman
sociology student must read. It is a question of who has
the right to peck whom and who must submit to being
pecked. There are only two important differences. The first
is that the pecking order is determined by the individual
strength and forcefulness of each chicken, whereas in the
White House it depends upon the relationship to the barnyard keeper. The second is that no one outside the barnyard glorifies the chickens and expects them to order the
affairs of mankind. They are destined for the frying pan and
that is that.

The White House does not provide an atmosphere in
which idealism and devotion can flourish. Below the president is a mass of intrigue, posturing, strutting, cringing,
and pious "commitment" to irrelevant windbaggery. It is
designed as the perfect setting for the conspiracy of medi-
ocrity—that all too frequently successful collection of the
untalented, the unpassionate, and the insincere seeking to
convince the public that it is brilliant, compassionate, and
dedicated.

There are, of course, men who seethe inwardly over
this affront to human dignity—most of whom either go
smash or leave quietly, their muscles set rigidly to contain
an indescribable agony. There are, of course, the warm and
relaxed permanent White House staff members, secure in
their mastery of the essential housekeeping machinery of
the mansion and watching with wry amusement and some

sympathy the frenetic efforts to shine forth boldly of those who have only four years out of all eternity to grab the brass ring. But the men of outrage are few and for some reason avoid each other after they slip out the side door. There are experiences which should not be shared. A reunion would lead only to a collective shriek.

It is not that the people who compose the ménage are any worse than any other collection of human beings. It is rather that the White House is an ideal cloak for intrigue, pomposity, and ambition. No nation of free men should ever permit itself to be governed from a hallowed shrine where the meanest lust for power can be sanctified and the dullest wit greeted with reverential awe. Government should be vulgar, sweaty, plebeian, operating in an environment where a fool can be called a fool and the motivations of ideological pimpery duly observed and noted. In a democracy, meanness, dullness, and corruption are entitled to representation because they are part of the human spirit; they are not entitled to protection from the harsh and rude challenges that such qualities must face in the real world.

It is not enough to say that the White House need not be like this if it is occupied by another set of personalities. It is not enough to point out that I may subconsciously be exaggerating the conditions which I describe in overreacting to the reverence that has characterized most studies of the presidency. The fact remains that the institution provides camouflage for all that is petty and nasty in human beings, and enables a clown or a knave to pose as Galahad and be treated with deference.

Is my reaction purely personal disappointment or shaped by service in a specific White House in a specific administration? Obviously, no man can be truly objective about an experience so central to his life and so vital to all his goals and his aspirations. All I can say is that I am fully aware of the treacherous nature of one's sensory mechanisms in surveying the immediately surrounding universe. I have taken this factor into account and tried to allow for it in every possible way—which is why this book has been so long delayed. I believe that what I am saying is more than the conclusion of one man in a unique set of circumstances.

The thirty years I have spent in Washington have been punctuated with a number of telltale incidents. I have observed, for example, that former White House assistants are reticent about their experiences. When pressed for a description they invariably resort to words like "richly rewarding" and "fulfilling"—the clichés that men always use when they wish to conceal, rather than to convey, thought. And their congratulations to newly appointed assistants begin always with perfunctory "best wishes" and then shift to heartfelt friendly tips on how to survive. Only once have I felt a genuine flash of fire. It came from one of the top "assistants with a passion for anonymity" of the Roosevelt days. I described to him White House life as I saw it and his response—which was passionate—was: "Don't worry! That's the way it has always been and that's the way it will always be!"

I have a feeling that Camelot was not a very happy place. Even the gentle language of Malory does not fully cloak hints of intrigue, corruption, and distrust —reaching as high as Guinevere. And the "Table Round" seems better adapted to boozing in a vain effort to drown disappointment than to knightly discourse on chivalrous deeds and weighty matters of state.

In fact, Malory makes virtually no effort to describe

Camelot as a seat of government. King Arthur was presumably beloved by his subjects because he was wise and valiant. But how did he handle roadbuilding, public charity, or the administration of justice? Such questions had to wait several hundred years for the advent of Mark Twain, whose entirely fictitious (and wholly irreverent) account was probably much closer to the reality than that produced by the original sources.

It is this aspect that gives cause for concern. The psychological ease of those who reside in Camelot does not matter except to the individuals themselves. But the type of government that Camelot produces affects every individual and, ultimately, can determine the character of the society in which we all must live.

It is my highly pessimistic view that Camelot will no longer suffice—however effective it may have been in the past. As a rallying point for men who would beat off dragons and ogres, it was superb. As a device to lead us through the stresses of modern life, it is wholly inadequate. And one of the few historical principles in which I still retain faith is that an inadequate government will either fall or resort to repression.

There is no reason to believe that the United States is exempt from the forces of history. We have no special writ from the Almighty which will substitute for normal human wisdom. There is no evidence that such wisdom is being applied effectively to the overwhelming problems that beset us nor is there any light on the horizon. And while it may seem premature at this point, we may well be witnessing the first lengthening of the shadows that will become the twilight of the presidency.

★

THE TWILIGHT OF THE PRESIDENCY

★

A president cannot have problems which are personal to him alone. His troubles are the troubles of the nation and if they become disastrous, the nation is in peril. It is vital, consequently, to identify those aspects of his position which are most likely to bring him to grief. And the most important, and least examined, problem of the presidency is that of maintaining contact with reality. Unless a president starts giving thought to this question—and on the available evidence, very few do—immediately following the fine flush of his election victory celebration, he is headed inevitably for trouble.

There are very few warnings to the president-elect that this problem will be encountered. No one has placed over the White House door the admonition *"facile decensus Averni."* No one comes rushing to him with somber warnings and Dutch-uncle talk. The state of euphoria induced by political success is upon him at the very moment that caution, introspection, and humility are most needed. The process of erosion by which reality gradually fades begins the moment someone says, "Congratulations, Mr. President."

There is built into the presidency a series of devices that tend to remove the occupant of the Oval Room from all of the forces which require most men to rub up against the hard facts of life on a daily basis. The life of the White House is the life of a court. It is a structure designed for one purpose and one purpose only—to serve the material needs and the desires of a single man. It is felt that this man is grappling with problems of such tremendous consequence that every effort must be made to relieve him of the irritations that vex the average citizen. His mind, it is held, must be absolutely free of petty annoyances so that he can concentrate his faculties upon the "great issues" of the day.

To achieve this end, every conceivable facility is made available, from the very latest and most luxurious jet aircraft to a masseur constantly in attendance to soothe raw presidential nerves. Even more important, however, he is treated with all of the reverence due a monarch. No one interrupts presidential contemplation for anything less than a major catastrophe somewhere on the globe. No one speaks to him unless spoken to first. No one ever invites him to "go soak your head" when his demands become petulant and unreasonable.

In theory, privilege is accorded to, and accepted by, a man in accordance with his responsibilities. It is a supposed compensation for heavier burdens than those carried by lesser mortals. In practice, privilege is a status that feeds upon itself—with every new perquisite automatically becoming a normal condition of life. Any president upon entering office is startled—and a little abashed—at the privileges that are available to him. But it is only a matter of months until they become part of an environment which he necessarily regards as his just and due entitlement—not because of the office but because of his mere existence.

It is doubtful whether even Harry S Truman—the most democratic of contemporary presidents—wore the same size hat when he left the White House as he did the day he entered.

This status was built into the American government by the Constitution itself. The founding fathers had rejected the concept of the divine right of monarchy. But when they sat down to write a constitution that would assure freedom, they were incapable of thinking of government in any terms other than monarchy. Someone, they reasoned, must reign and rule. Someone must give orders that could not be questioned. Someone must have ultimate and final authority. Therefore, their conclusion, although not stated in these terms, was a solution which placed in office a monarch but limited the scope of the monarch's activities.

In the context of the late eighteenth century, the solution was an excellent one. First, the founding fathers analyzed the functions of the government and divided them into three basic categories—the determination of policy, the execution of policy, and the adjudication of disputes arising out of the determination and the execution. The determination of policy was granted to Congress and the adjudication of disputes to the judiciary. The execution of policy they lodged in the hands of the president and within that area they gave him, for all practical purposes, total authority, not so much by affirmation but by failing to set many boundaries on what he could do. They felt that by dividing functions they had created competing power centers within the government and that the competition would prevent any one center from assuming a complete monopoly of power. As an additional safeguard, they limited the term of the president to four years (with an option for renewal if mutually agreeable between the president and the electorate) and gave Congress the authority to remove the president from office, although only on the basis of cumbersome machinery.

The accent was on stability and the firebrands of the Revolution—Tom Paine, Patrick Henry, James Otis—were given short shrift, the traditional fate of revolutionaries when men meet to put the pieces together after the crockery has been smashed. But the founding fathers were neither reactionary nor timorous. They provided—whether consciously, intuitively, or by sheer luck—ample room for the constitutional institutions to react in new ways to new circumstances, as long as the institutions themselves did not change in any fundamental respect. Generally, this objective was achieved by indirection.

The president, for example, was forbidden to legislate or adjudicate, but there was remarkably little definition of his executive powers. As a result, the size of the president in office at any given time determined the extent of what he regarded as his mandate. It was inevitable that strong men such as Jackson, Lincoln, and the two Roosevelts would interpret the absence of specific prohibitions as the presence of specific authority and act accordingly. Harry S Truman even invoked the doctrine of "inherent" presidential powers to seize the nation's steel mills despite the lack of any legislative authorization—an effort that did not succeed because his popular following at the time was far short of his own supply of willpower.

Of equal importance was the failure to provide a method of determining whether acts of Congress transgressed the permissible boundaries of the Constitution. It was inevitable that such questions would arise and would be regarded differently by men whose function was to represent the popular will and men whose function was to administer a theoretically impersonal body of law. Had the doctrine of judicial review of legislative acts not been established by John Marshall, it is virtually certain that one of his successors would have done so. This particular gap was so huge that it had to be plugged somehow. But it is only a matter of time until a body which has succeeded in acquiring the power to forbid (which is essentially the power of the Supreme Court over Congress and the executive) also takes over the power to direct. This is the process that has made the judiciary a major agency for social change in the past two decades.

The framers of the Constitution had no way of foreseeing the effects of their most important decision—to give the presidency the functions of both chief of state and chief of government. It is doubtful whether they were aware at the time that the functions could exist separately. They knew that there had to be someone who spoke for all the government. They also knew that there had to be someone to manage the affairs of the country. The concept that these two functions could be separated was alien to their experience, even though the origins of separation were already apparent in the relationship between the king of England and the English prime minister.

They lived in a universe dominated by the concept of ownership and in which management independent of ownership was unknown. The parallel to government seemed obvious in their minds. Furthermore, they were confronted with an immediate and apparent problem which far overshadowed what could then only be abstract ideas of the distinction between reigning and ruling. They had a nation which was being pulled apart by the centrifugal forces of state pride. Their task was to devise some method by which thirteen quite independent political units could be merged into a collective whole. Their problem was to find some counterweight that would balance forces of disunity and induce Americans to think of themselves as citizens of the United States rather than as citizens of Connecticut, New York, Virginia, or Georgia.

The most practical method of unifying people is to give them a symbol with which all can identify. If the symbol is human, its efficacy is enhanced enormously. The obvious symbol was the president—the man who held the role of commander-in-chief of the armed forces; the man to whom all could pay respects as the first citizen. In short, the founding fathers established the presidency as a position of reverence and, as they were truly wise and sophisticated men, their efforts were as effective as human wisdom could make them.

The consequences of this decision were ultimately inescapable although not immediately discernible. In the simple society of the eighteenth-century United States, it was not easy to conceive of the Federal government in terms of grandeur. An Abigail Adams could hang her washing in the East Room; a Dolly Madison could act as a porter, running to safety with important works of art in advance of British occupation; an Andrew Jackson could invite all his frontier friends into the White House for a rollicking party where they could trample the official furniture with muddy boots and pass out dead drunk on the plush carpets of the Oval Room. But even in a nation as close to the realities of the frontier as the United States, a position established to inspire awe and reverence would inevitably pick up the trappings of reverence. And the trappings could not fail to have an effect upon the man whom they served as a buffer against the rest of the world.

Among the fundamental characteristics of monarchy is untouchability. Contact with the king is forbidden except to an extremely few people or as a rare privilege to be exercised on great occasions. The king's body is sanctified and not subject to violation by lesser mortals unless he himself so wishes. He is not to be jostled in crowds; he is not to be clapped on the back; he is not to be placed in danger of life or limb or even put to the annoyance of petty physical discomfort. Nor can he be compelled to account for his actions upon demand.

By the twentieth century, the presidency had taken on all the regalia of monarchy except ermine robes, a scepter, and a crown. The president was not to be jostled by a crowd—unless he elected to subject himself to do so during those moments when he shed his role as chief of state and mounted the hustings as a candidate for re-election. The ritual of shaking hands with the president took on more and more the coloration of the medieval "king's touch" as a specific for scrofula. The president was not to be called to account by any other body (after the doctrine of executive privilege was established). In time, another kingly habit began to appear and presidents referred to themselves more and more as "we"—the ultimate hallmark of imperial majesty.

These are the conditions under which a president-elect enters office in the modern era. In fact, the aura of majesty begins to envelop him the moment it becomes apparent that the electorate has decided upon its next president. Trusted assistants who have been calling him by his first name for many years switch immediately to the deferential "Mr. President." The Secret Service agents who have been protecting him during the campaign are suddenly joined by their chiefs who, up to that point, have stayed away from him and the other candidates in order to emphasize their neutrality. Members of the Army Signal Corps almost silently appear with communications equipment such as he has never seen before. All these developments take place as he bathes in the universal congratulations that always come to the successful candidate, even from his bitterest opponents. The agents that corrupt the democratic soul creep into his life in the guise of enthusiastic supporters, tactful policemen, self-effacing telephone linemen, and well-trained house servants. Even the members of the press, for a few months at least, regard him with some awe. The apotheosis has begun.

During the early days of a president's incumbency, the atmosphere of reverence which surrounds him acquires validity in his own eyes because of the ease with which he can get results. Congress is eager to approve his nominees and pass his bills. Business is anxious to provide him with "friends" and assistants. Labor is ready to oblige him with a climate of industrial peace. Foreign ambassadors scurry to locate suitable approaches.

It is a wonderful and heady feeling to be a president— at least for the first few months.

The environment of deference, approaching sycophancy, helps to foster another insidious factor. It is a belief that the president and a few of his most trusted advisers are possessed of a special knowledge which must be closely held within a small group lest the plans and the designs of the United States be anticipated and frustrated by enemies. It is a knowledge which is thought to be endangered in geometrical proportion to the number of other men to whom it is passed. Therefore, the most vital national projects can be worked out only within a select coterie, or there will be a "leak" which will disadvantage the country's security.

Obviously, there *is* information which a nation must keep to itself if it is to survive in the present world climate. This means that the number of minds which can be brought to bear on any given problem is often in inverse proportion to the importance of the problem.

The steps that led to the bombing of North Vietnam were all discussed by a small group of men. They were intelligent men—men of keen perception and finely honed judgment. It is doubtful whether any higher degree of intelligence could have been brought to bear on the problem. But no matter how fine the intelligence or how thoroughgoing the information available, the fact remained that none of these men was put to the test of defending his position in public debate. And it is amazing what even the best of minds will discover when forced to answer critical questions. Unfortunately, in this as in many other instances, the need to comment publicly came after, and not before, irreversible commitment.

Of course, within these councils there was always at least one "devil's advocate." But an official dissenter always starts with half his battle lost. It is assumed that he is bringing up arguments solely because arguing is his official role. It is well understood that he is not going to press his points harshly or stridently. Therefore, his objections and cautions are discounted before they are delivered. They are actually welcomed because they prove for the record that decision was preceded by controversy.

As a general rule, the quality of judgment usually varies directly with the number of minds that are brought to bear upon an issue. No man is so wise as to play his own "devil's advocate," and workable wisdom is the distillation of many different viewpoints which have clashed heatedly and directly in an exchange of opinion. To maintain the necessary balance between assurances of security and assurances that enough factors have been taken into consideration is perhaps the most pressing problem of statecraft. The atmosphere of the White House, in which the president is treated constantly as an infallible and reverential object, is not the best in which to resolve this problem.

In retrospect, it seems little short of amazing that President Kennedy would ever have embarked upon the ill-fated Bay of Pigs venture. It was poorly conceived, poorly planned, poorly executed, and undertaken with grossly inadequate knowledge. But anyone who has ever sat in on a White House council can easily deduce what happened without knowing any facts other than those which appeared in the public press. White House councils are not debating matches in which ideas emerge from the heated exchanges of participants. The council centers around the president himself, to whom everyone addresses his observations.

The first strong observations to attract the favor of the president become subconsciously the thoughts of everyone in the room. The focus of attention shifts from a testing of all concepts to a groping for means of overcoming the difficulties. A thesis which could not survive an undergraduate seminar in a liberal-arts college becomes accepted doctrine, and the only question is not *whether* it should be done but *how* it should be done. A forceful public airing of the Bay of Pigs plan would have endangered the whole project, of course. But it might have prevented disaster.

On a different level can be cited the far less serious setback suffered by President Lyndon B. Johnson when he attempted to merge the Commerce and the Labor departments into one agency. Out of a desire for a "surprise" headline, this proposal was held in the utmost secrecy between the president and his speech writers until a few moments before his State of the Union message was scheduled for delivery. Quick calls were made to the secretaries of labor and commerce, who were pressed for a quick response and who reacted as any government official reacts to such a call from the White House. They said, "Yes."

In a matter of days, it was apparent that the project had as much chance of getting off the ground as a kiwi. To organized labor, still headed by men with long memories, the Labor Department was a sacrosanct institution for which they had fought and bled in their youth. They had no intention of acquiescing to the removal from the cabinet of what they regarded as "our spokesman." Business, while far less emotional, made it quite clear that industrialists did not relish the prospect of "our agency" being merged with what they regarded as the opposition. The president quietly buried the whole idea.

The truly baffling question, however, is how a man with the political sensitivity of Lyndon B. Johnson would ever embark on such a futile enterprise. The basis of his success as the Senate Democratic leader had been his insistence upon touching every base before launching a project. He was famous throughout the political community for "taking the temperature" of every affected group in advance and laying careful plans to meet any objections they might have before the objections were even raised. And yet here was an instance where even a perfunctory conversation with a few of his friends would have made clear that humiliation was the only conceivable outcome of his proposal.

The only conclusion that an observer can draw is that the atmosphere of the White House—the combination of sycophancy and a belief in the efficacy of closely held knowledge—had done its work. The man regarded as the outstanding politician of the mid-twentieth century had stepped into a buzzsaw which could have been foreseen by a wardheeler in any major city of America.

A reader of history will find innumerable and startling examples of political bloopers committed by men with a record of political sagacity. How is one to explain President Truman's inept handling of the Communist spy scare of the late 1940s—a mistake which opened up the era of Joe McCarthy? How is one to explain Franklin D. Roosevelt's futile effort to "pack" the Supreme Court? How is one to explain Woodrow Wilson's clumsy treatment of the Senate, which led directly to its refusal to permit United States participation in the League of Nations? None of these men had shown themselves politically inept on such a grand scale at any previous moment of their lives. It is only an inference but an inescapable one that the White House is an institution which dulls the sensitivity of political men and ultimately reduces them to bungling amateurs in their basic craft—the art of politics.

The real question every president must ask himself is what he can do to resist the temptations of a process compounded of idolatry and lofty patriotic respect for a national symbol. By all the standards of past performance, he should be well equipped to face it. As a general rule, he has fought his way up through the political ranks. He has flattered and been flattered—and the mere fact that he has survived to the threshold of the White House should indicate a psychological capacity to keep flattery in perspective. He has dealt with rich people, poor people, wise men, fools, patriots, knaves, scoundrels, and wardheelers. Had he not maintained his perspective on human beings generally, it is doubtful that he would ever have received his party's nomination.

But the atmosphere of the White House is a heady one. It is designed to bring to its occupant privileges that are commensurate in scope with the responsibilities that he must bear. A privilege is, by definition, a boon not accorded to other people. And to the extent that a man exercises his privileges, he removes himself from the company of lesser breeds who must stand in line and wait their turn on a share-and-share-alike basis for the comforts of life. To a president, all other humans are "lesser breeds."

Furthermore, a president would have to be a dull clod indeed to regard himself without a feeling of awe. The atmosphere of the White House is calculated to instill in any man a sense of destiny. He literally walks in the footsteps of hallowed figures—of Jefferson, of Jackson, of Lincoln. The almost sanctified relics of a distant, semimythical past surround him as ordinary household objects to be used by his family. From the moment he enters the halls he is made aware that he has become enshrined in a pantheon of semidivine mortals who have shaken the world, and that he has taken from their hands the heritage of American dreams and aspirations.

Unfortunately for him, divinity is a better basis for inspiration than it is for government. The world can be shaken from Mount Olympus but the gods were notoriously inefficient when it came to directing the affairs of mankind. The Greeks were wise about such matters. In their remarkable body of lore, human tragedy usually originated with divine intervention and their invocations to the deities were usually prayers of propitiation—by all that is holy, leave us alone!

A semidivinity is also a personification of a people, and presidents cannot escape the process. The trouble with personification is that it depends upon abstraction and, in the course of the exercise, individual living people somehow get lost. The president becomes the nation and when he is insulted, the nation is insulted; when he has a dream, the nation has a dream; when he has an antagonist, the nation has an antagonist.

The purpose of this book is to examine the effects of this environment upon the president of the United States. This has become a matter of great urgency. It is increasingly evident that the tasks of the presidency are more and more demanding. It is also increasingly evident that presidents spend more of their time swimming in boiling political waters. There is even a respectable body of thought which holds that the problems are out of control and that, in the present context, the nation must look forward to a series of one-term presidents, incapable of holding the office for more than four years.

As a general rule, efforts to remedy the deficiencies of the presidency center on proposals to bring a greater administrative efficiency to the White House itself. It is held that the problems would become manageable if the president had better tools at his command. In my mind there is a strong suspicion that the problems are no more unmanageable today than they have been in the past. They are, of course, bigger in terms of consequence. But they are still decision rather than management problems. Perhaps a more fruitful path lies in an exploration of the extent to which the atmosphere of the White House degrades a man's political instincts and abilities. Our thoughts should be centered not on electronic brains but on the forces that would foster the oldest, the noblest, and the most vital of all human arts—the art of politics.

★

One of the American people's most cherished notions about the presidency is that the office somehow ennobles the occupant and renders him fit to meet any crisis. This concept probably achieved its most articulate expression in a book and a movie, *Gabriel Over the White House* (now mercifully forgotten), which was the favorite reading and viewing of millions during the early days of the New Deal.

Those who hold this idea are fond of referring to Harry S Truman and his unexpected rise (as they see it) from a small-town machine politician to a world statesman possessed of rare qualities of courage and high purpose. They are less fond, of course, of references to Warren G. Harding and Calvin Coolidge who left the presidency looking very little, if any, different than they did when they entered office.

It is a thesis of this book that the office neither elevates nor degrades a man. What it does is to provide a stage upon which all of his personality traits are magnified and accentuated. The aspects of his character which were not noted previously are not really new. They were merely hidden from view in lesser positions, where he was only one of many politicians competing for public attention. It is absurd to contend that Mr. Truman's great courage and patriotism—the most noteworthy of his attributes—came to him when he walked into the Oval Room. The truth— which would be borne out by all of his intimates—is that he always possessed such qualities. But who would notice them in a senator from Missouri—particularly a senator who cared little about the techniques of public relations?

A president is one of the few figures in political life who will not be regarded in terms of stereotypes. A senator who comes to Washington is very quickly put into the class of liberal, conservative, or moderate (the latter usually meaning nondescript). These terms are not truly descriptive of his political ideology but of the symbols which he uses. The stereotypes are useful because without them it would be difficult for the press to analyze events. But they have a tendency to obscure the man. Lyndon Johnson's espousal of civil rights and welfare legislation as president came as a surprise to many people simply because they had spent a number of years looking at a label rather than a person. And Dwight D. Eisenhower's warning against the military-industrial complex seemed out of character simply because of the popular mythology that had portrayed him as a well-meaning but not overly bright general. Neither of the men actually changed when he entered the White House. Nobody had really looked at him before.

In actuality, a man's character and personality are not of the same concern in relation to his role as a senator or a member of the House of Representatives as they are to the role of the presidency. In Congress he is only one of a large group of advocates, and the end product of his activities will be tempered by his need for arriving at an accommodation with the others.

Presidential performance is a totally different matter. In the White House, character and personality are extremely important because there are no other limitations which govern a man's conduct. Restraint must come from within the presidential soul and prudence from within the presidential mind. The adversary forces which temper the actions of others do not come into play until it is too late to change course.

Richard E. Neustadt has observed that expertise in presidential power "seems to be the province not of politicians as a class but of extraordinary politicians." The point is well taken and this writer suggests only a minor modification. The last few words should read "extraordinary *men* who have become politicians." This suggestion is put forward only because it is essential to this chapter to emphasize the crucial importance of personality to the success of a president.

Before plunging too deeply into the problem of the president and reality, it might be well to explore briefly what a president does—or at least what he should do. This exploration is particularly essential at this time because of the widespread impression that the president is an overworked man and that the principal problem of the presidency is to devise administrative structures which will conserve his time and permit him to operate more efficiently. It is this common impression which has led to a series of proposals that part of the workload be transferred to the vice-president or even that there be two or more vice-presidents dividing foreign and domestic affairs.

Despite the widespread belief to the contrary, however, there is far less to the presidency, in terms of essential activity, than meets the eye. The psychological burdens are heavy, even crushing, but no president ever died of over-work and it is doubtful whether any ever will. The chief executive can, of course, fill his working hours with as much motion as he desires. The "crisis" days (the rebellion in the Dominican Republic or the attempted torpedoing of American navy vessels in the Gulf of Tonkin) can keep office lights burning into the mid-night hours. But in terms of actual administrative work, the presidency is pretty much what the president wants to make of it. He can delegate the "work" to subordinates and reserve for himself only the powers of decision as did Dwight D. Eisenhower or he can insist upon maintaining tight control over every minor detail, like Lyndon B. John-son.

The concept of the president who works around the clock is deep in American mythology, however, and, with the exception of President Eisenhower, presidents have agreed that it must be maintained. Even in the case of President Eisenhower, his assistants thought they had to keep up appearances regardless of their chief's disdain for dissimulation. Jim Haggerty, his press secretary, was no-torious for "saving up" official papers and announcements to release while the president was on vacation—thus pre-serving the illusion that it was a combination work-and-play holiday.

This has led to the now venerable tradition in the press office of preparing a "day in the life of the president" for handling the queries of reporters burdened with this story by somewhat unsophisticated editors. It is, of course, usually labeled a "typical" day in the life of the president, with the date unspecified. Care must be taken not to put two major and well-publicized events together in the list so

that someone will spot a discrepancy (i.e., don't combine a major announcement of more troops for Vietnam
with an important—and announced—meeting of the
National Security Council that happened two weeks later).
A press secretary scratching for a believable schedule
quickly finds out how few "working" events actually take
place and usually falls back on a day when the president
received, and accepted the credentials of, ten ambassadors
(three minutes each) and inserts into the list "worked at
his desk for three hours."

Another measurement of the "workload" can be found
in the long-standing custom of the White House press office
of scouring the executive agencies for items to release
to the newspaper correspondents. It is a practice which
has led generations of information officers to the verge of
rebellion because of the obvious fact that if an item is unknown *to* the White House in the normal course of events,
it is probably an item which should not be released *from*
the White House anyway. Nevertheless, the practice has
continued and newspapermen have found themselves
bombarded on a daily basis with releases on waterfowl
conservation, minor grants for pollution abatement, and
education projects for Indian reservations. Such releases
rarely make headlines but their sheer bulk creates the
impression of unending activity on the part of the president.

The concept of the overburdened president represents one of the insidious forces which serve to separate
the chief executive from the real universe of living, breath-
ing, troubled human beings. It is the basis for encourag-
ing his most outrageous expressions, for pampering his
most childish tantrums, for fostering his most arrogant actions. More than anything else, it serves to create an en-

vironment in which no man can live for any considerable length of time and retain his psychological balance.

A president can be rude, insulting, and even down-right sadistic to his closest advisers and their only response will be: "How fortunate that he has people around him who understand the tremendous burdens he is carrying." He can display the social manners of a Vandal sacking a Roman villa and his intimates will remark to each other: "We don't care about style. The only thing that is important is his deep feeling for the urban poor. Of course, he is somewhat crude but what does that matter?" He can ele-vate a mediocre sycophant to high position and members of his entourage will remark to each other: "You know, it is amazing how perceptive and socially conscious that young man is!"

The burdens would be lighter, the urban poor would be better served, and the young men might be more ·per-ceptive and socially conscious if presidents had to face the same minor social penalties that the rest of us do. An occasional "go soak your head" or "that's stupid" would clear the murky, turgid atmosphere of the White House and let in some health-giving fresh air.

This, however, is not a likelihood. A president moves through his days surrounded by literally hundreds of peo-ple whose relationship to him is that of a doting mother to a spoiled child. Whatever he wants is brought to him im-mediately—food, drink, helicopters, airplanes, people, in fact, everything but relief from his political problems. And the assistant who is unable to provide a requested service—no matter how unreasonable—automatically blames him-self for his shortcomings rather than external circum-stances.

The system feeds upon itself. Impossible demands which cannot be met breed guilt feelings which serve as a basis for rationalizing even more impossible demands. It is little wonder that former White House assistants need a period of decompression, in which they can re-establish their own egos, even more than does the president, after they leave office.

The presidential burden, of course, does not lie in the workload. It stems from the crushing responsibility of political decision, with life and death literally hanging in the balance for hundreds of millions of people. A president is haunted every waking hour of his life by the fear that he has taken the wrong turn, selected the wrong course, issued the wrong orders. In the realm of political decision he can turn to no one for *authoritative counsel.* Only *he* is authoritative. The situation was summed up by Harry S Truman in the sign he kept on his desk, "The Buck Stops Here."

Every reflective human being eventually realizes that the heaviest burdens of his life are not the responsibilities he bears for himself but the responsibilities he bears for others. Where the load becomes too heavy, he can walk out easily if no one else is affected. The escape process becomes more difficult when his family is involved. And as the number of people dependent upon him increases, it becomes virtually impossible. The president's responsibilities literally embrace—either positively or negatively—every living person. There is no escape—no place to hide—not even for a moment.

Those who seek to lighten the burdens of the presidency by easing the workload do no occupant of that office a favor. The "workload"—and especially the ceremonial workload—are the only events of a president's day which make life endurable. They are the only occasions that give him an opportunity to concentrate his mental processes on problems which are amenable to technical solution—and thereby blot out of his consciousness the image of napalm exploding through the houses of an Asian village at his order; of hungry people walking the streets because he might have misused his fiscal authority; of angry opponents sharpening political knives in anticipation of revenge for a slight which he inflicted in a moment of irritation; of jeering cartoons and sneering slogans held aloft on giant placards by college youth alienated because he increased the draft quotas. *Work* is a blessed relief which comes all too rarely.

It is difficult to pinpoint this phenomenon, as it does not yield readily to quantitative analysis. It is not possible to really take a day and divide it with any sure sense of confidence into "working hours" and "nonworking hours." But it is apparent from the large volume of words that have been written about presidents that in the past few decades, the only one who seemed able to relax completely was Dwight D. Eisenhower. He was fully capable of taking a vacation for the sake of enjoying his vacation, and he was totally disdainful of any suggestion that he was acting otherwise. In his first year in office, Mr. Nixon is giving evidence of emulating Mr. Eisenhower, if the reports from California present a true picture. However, it will take some time to determine whether this is his real attitude or whether he is presenting a deliberate image of a relaxed president.

Franklin D. Roosevelt apparently had little or no time to devote to sheer relaxation. He was notorious for using his dinner hours as a means of lobbying bills through Congress. Harry S Truman was able to put a decision that had been made out of his mind and proceed to another problem. Furthermore, he too disdained any pretensions of working when he wasn't. But those who were close to him make it quite clear that he really didn't know what to do with himself when he took a holiday. His favorite vacation resort was Key West, Florida, where he would "go fishing"—but obviously he would only hold a rod if someone put it in his hands and about all he really enjoyed was the sunshine and the opportunity to take long walks.

President Kennedy was described as a "compulsive reader" who could not pass up any written document regardless of its relevance to his problems or even of its general contents. It was reported by many of his intimates that any spare time would find him restlessly prowling the White House looking for something to scan. Lyndon Johnson looked forward with horror to the long weekends in which there was really nothing to do. The result was usually a Saturday afternoon spent in lengthy conferences with individual newspapermen who would be hastily summoned from their homes and would spend hours with him while he expounded the thesis that his days were so taken up with the nation's business that he had no time to devote to friends.

The real misery of the average presidential day is the haunting sense that decisions have been made on incomplete information and inadequate counsel. Tragically, the information must *always* be incomplete and the counsel *always* inadequate, for the arena of human activity in which a president operates is one in which there are no quantitative answers. He must deal with those problems for which the computer offers no solution; those disputes where rights and wrongs are so inextricably mixed that the right-ing of every wrong creates a new wrong; those divisions which arise out of differences in human desires rather than differences in the available facts; those crisis moments in which action is so imperative that it cannot wait upon orderly consideration. He has no guideposts other than his own philosophy and his intuition, and if he is devoid of either, no one can substitute. Other people can tell him "what I would do if I were president." But those other people are *not* president. Try as they may, they cannot achieve that sense of personal identification with history which is the hallmark of the chief executive. Presidents are wont to explain those of their decisions which are incomprehensible to their contemporaries on the grounds that they have access to information not available in its entirety to other men. The inference is: "If you knew what I knew, you would understand why I did what I did." That a president has more comprehensive data available to him is true (or at least can be true if a president pays sufficient attention to his sources of information) but is actually irrelevant. On sweeping policy decisions, which are, after all, relatively few, a president makes up his mind on the basis of the same *kind* of information that is available to the average citizen. When Franklin D. Roosevelt decided to commit this nation against the Axis powers he had little relevant information on the Nazis, the Fascists, and the Japanese warlords that was qualitatively different from that which could be gleaned from the *New York Times*. When Harry Truman decided to resist Communist aggression in Korea, he knew very little more than that the Forty-ninth Parallel had been crossed by Communist troops, a fact which was already in headlines. When Lyndon Johnson decided to send troops into the Dominican Republic, he had no information advantage over his fellow Americans

other than a brief telephone conversation with his ambassador (although later reams of factual data were gathered to justify the action).

Of course, a president usually *knows* more about the
situation than other people—not because he has more information but because it is his *business* to know and men
usually pay attention to their business. He has the responsibility of making ultimate decisions which will be
submitted to the harshest judgment possible—the judgment of history. This is the kind of prospect that tends
to concentrate a man's mind wonderfully.

Moreover, the difference in the decision-making process between the president and his fellow Americans is not
necessarily that he has taken better advantage of the available facts than they have but that he, and only he, must
make the decision. As it is his business to *know*, it is his
exclusive business to *decide*. This gives his thought processes a quality which no other person, not even his most
trusted adviser, can have. His fellow Americans stand in
the position of critics. They can "second guess"; they can
be "Monday morning quarterbacks." Quite possibly they
will have judgments demonstrably superior to those made
by the president. But they do not have to say "yes" or
"no" under the pressure of a deadline. They do not have to
concern themselves about the prospect that history may
damn them eternally. They do not have to take responsibility for action in the sure knowledge that the action will
produce consequences which will demonstrate to the
whole world that they were right or wrong. Neither do
they have to offer leadership to diverse groups of people
who are strong-willed and convinced of their own right-
eousness.

A president is many things. The demands of his office

call upon him to be a symbol of the nation, to be a teacher, to be a political organizer, to be a moral preceptor, to be an arbiter of taste. But what he must do, in order to earn his keep, can be boiled down to two simple fundamentals. He must resolve the policy questions that will not yield to quantitative, empirical analyses; and he must persuade enough of his countrymen of the rightness of his decisions so that he can carry them out without destroying the fabric of society.

Neither of these functions can be discharged by anyone other than the president. None of the analytical techniques of social science have yet replaced the intuitive judgment of a politician as to the time and place for taking certain steps. And even should such analytical techniques be devised, it is inconceivable that any president would surrender his judgment to them. The electorate places in the White House a man—not an electronic computer.

The difference between the great and the mediocre presidents probably centers on the individual ability of each one to grasp this point. The great presidents understood the White House as a focal point of power from which could flow the decisions that shaped the destiny of the nation. They realized that the day-to-day activities of a president were intended to bolster support for policies, to obtain the backing that could translate their intuitive judgment into meaningful action, and to deal with the conflicting forces that lie within our society in such a way that they could be reduced to common denominators and therefore to a degree of coherence. The mediocre presidents, on the other hand, have tended to regard the White House as a stage for the presentation of performances to the public or as a fitting honor to cap a career that was illustrious in some other field.

It is doubtful whether Franklin D. Roosevelt made a single speech as president which did not have a specific political objective. Sometimes his timing was wrong (as in the 1934 "quarantine the aggressors" speech in which he unsuccessfully tried to lead the nation out of isolationism). Sometimes his timing was superb (as was his "little dog Fala" speech, which blasted his Republican opponent out of the presidential race in 1944). But always there was an objective—a reason for making a speech other than a display of rhetoric.

It is not my intention here to name and label the mediocre presidents. But the reader is invited to inspect the speeches made by those whom he considers in that category. It will become quickly apparent that most of these speeches were made solely for the occasion rather than for their impact.

A brief look should be taken at the nature of decision making in the White House. Upon few other governmental subjects have so many words been lavished. It is assumed that there is something called a "decision-making process" which can be charted in much the same fashion as the table of organization for a business corporation. The fondest dream of the academic political scientist is to trace this flow chart in such a way that it will be available for study, comment, criticism, and possibly improvement. It may be that such a process existed during the administration of Dwight D. Eisenhower. Certainly, this was a widespread impression at the time. It was stated by writer after writer that "Ike" had introduced the military staff-and-command system to the presidency and that a filtering process examined all the options and eventually presented them to him in the form of a one-page paper upon which he could inscribe "yes" or "no." This has been repeated so many times and so little disputed that it is probably a fact, although anyone who has had White House service will forever after be skeptical of the pictures that are painted on the outside. But if so, it was a development which has occurred only once in recent years.

The fact is that a president makes his decisions as he wishes to make them, under conditions which he himself has established, and at times of his own determination. He decides what he wants to decide and any student of the White House who believes that he is making a contribution to political thought when he analyzes the process is sadly mistaken. At best—at the very best—he can only contribute to human knowledge some insights into the decision-making process of one man.

Presidents glory in telling people that they are prisoners of a system and of circumstances beyond their control. This is probably the subconscious device by which the chief executive prepares his alibi for history. It is true that they must deal with forces and circumstances which they did not create and which they cannot ignore. But how they deal with them is up to the presidents themselves. A president, in a peculiar sense that does not apply to other people, is the master of his own fate and the captain of his own soul. If Congress is balky, this is a political problem and a president is supposedly a political expert. If information is inadequate, the president has at his command a Federal establishment of at least 2,500,000 people over which he has virtually undisputed authority. If foreign relations are contentious and unruly, this is merely one of the conditions under which he operates and not a "reason" for failure.

There was no categorical imperative which required McKinley to declare war on Spain, Woodrow Wilson to serve an ultimatum on Germany, John F. Kennedy to order the invasion of the Bay of Pigs, or Lyndon Johnson to increase American forces in Vietnam from 20,000 to 500,-000. These were all decisions made by human beings who had other options. Whether they were right or wrong is another matter which will not be discussed here. The only truly relevant point is that none of these presidents was a prisoner of history at the crucial moment of truth. They may have been prisoners of psychological forces in their childhood, of racial and ethnic memories, of environments which molded their thinking and conditioned their reflexes. But whatever psychic forces may have been playing upon them, they could all have said "no."

This is a point well worth bearing in mind. The essence of the presidency is the responsibility for making decisions and the necessity for making them without peers —with advice and counsel, yes; but also in the sure knowledge that the president alone bears the full and complete burden.

★

III | THE PRESIDENTIAL GAMBIT

B efore examining the sources and nature of presidential power, it would be well to inquire briefly into the question of political power itself. This is a matter which is very little understood—perhaps because it is taken for granted after so many centuries of human history in which power rested upon divine sanction and was not to be questioned except on the basis of a superior divinity.

The basis of power is persuasion, even in an allegedly absolute dictatorship. The absolute dictator does not have to persuade a majority of the people over whom he rules that he should have the right to do so. But he must persuade some of the people who have the instruments of power—the army, the police, the clergy—to support him and exercise their means of compulsion in his behalf. There is no form of government that does not depend upon some such means of persuasion and there has not been such a form since human beings arose above the one-to-one relationship in which the stronger person could prevail by sheer force of muscle.

Even a superficial analysis of the dictatorships at work in the world indicates clearly that the most absolute despots are compelled to court and hold the loyalty of some group in their society. Fully untrammeled rule exists only in the popular imagination. In Haiti, for example, the strength of Dr. Duvalier rests upon the allegiance of the Tonton Macoutes, without whom he would be toppled quickly. Fidel Castro depends upon the Cuban cane cutters who, if they turned against him, could unseat the bearded dictator in the course of an afternoon. In more complicated countries, such as the Soviet Union, there may be alternative sources of power and in this instance a limited form of democracy exists at the top level. For many decades, Soviet politics has rested upon the capacity of a leader or a group of leaders to gain the allegiance of two of the three major sources of power—the army, the secret police, the Communist party. The Communist hierarchy can rule the great mass of Russian people with only a minimum amount of attention to their needs and desires. But it cannot ignore those who make up the membership of the three powerful organizations, and, to the extent that these organizations differ in their objectives, both change and a limited amount of freedom are possible.

The theory of democracy is that power shall reside in the people and that they shall have an opportunity to register their desires at periodic intervals. But since the mood of the people is subject to repeated and unforeseen changes, the great problem has always been to combine the necessary continuing authority to rule with the necessary checks to prevent that rule from becoming despotic. The contribution of the men who wrote the American Constitution was the thesis that power could be divided and lodged in different institutions—the executive, the legislative, the judiciary—in such a way that no one of these institutions could ever gain a monopoly. The success of this thesis has been little short of amazing in that the United States has remained a reasonably democratic nation since 1789. But it is equally interesting that, in the process of history, the American government has undergone changes which have taken it far from the concepts set forth by the men of Philadelphia. The most interesting change has been in the power and the authority of the president.

The men who wrote the Constitution very obviously ascribed to the president a lesser role than the legislative in the field of policy. It was clear that he would manage the affairs of the government, both military and civil, and that he would represent the United States in its dealings with other nations. But his management was assumed to be within limits laid down by legislation; and in dealing with other nations what he represented was supposed to be determined by Congress. There was little realization that his role as an activist would place the president in an advantageous position from which his domination of the Federal establishment became an inevitability.

In our managerial-oriented society, where administrative techniques have been raised to the status of an intellectual discipline in leading universities, we are all conscious of the direct relationship between the capacity to launch action and the control over the instruments and resources which make the action possible. To us it is self-evident that the chief executive officer, who administers payrolls, the collection and disbursement of funds, and the activities of production and sales, will determine the policies of a corporation until he is replaced by a successor. He can be harassed by stockholders, his life can be made difficult by an unfriendly board of directors. But even though the stockholders, and their representatives on the board of directors, can cause a shift in policy by firing their chief executive officer and bringing in a replacement, it is still *the new man* who will make corporate policy. Presumably, he will take into account the forces that placed him in office. But the extent to which he *must* do so is determined only by his political skill. And he is in a position almost daily to make commitments for the corporation of such a nature that the stockholders and directors have little alternative other than to acquiesce. They can, of course, get rid of him but this is a step that is usually taken only when provocation is extreme. Once he has his basic budget approved, he has the power of initiative—the power to initiate lawsuits, specific expenditures, sales campaigns, and new production models, and all these steps have self-perpetuating forces built into them. It is entirely possible for any corporate manager to lead his firm in a direction diametrically opposite from that intended by his stockholders without abusing any of his authority or usurping any undue prerogatives. He can do it merely by day-to-day decisions which *must* be made by someone and which *cannot* be made by a committee.

This concept was not very clear to the founding fathers. They thought of usurpation of power only in terms of bad law, ignored law, or violated law. They felt that the capacity of human reasoning to determine or alter human destiny was limited only by the quality of the intellects that could be brought to bear, by the physical environment, and by the relative balance of coercive powers in a society. As sophisticated men, they had little faith in human wisdom but thought it was perfectible through discussion. They accepted the physical environment philosophically as having both advantages and disadvantages (difficult trade routes from Europe to the New World were also difficult invasion routes). And they sought to create a balance of coercive powers which would cancel each other out. Their reaction was both rational and adequate to the times. No one then could have foreseen the rise of our interdependent society with its almost minute division of labor creating social forces that have a life of their own.

They made the president commander-in-chief of the armed forces. But they counterbalanced this power by lodging in the Congress the authority to raise and support those forces and by guaranteeing the people the inviolable right to bear arms.

They made the president the sole spokesman in the field of foreign affairs. But they counterbalanced this power by lodging in the Senate the sole right to pass upon the validity of treaties.

They made the president responsible for staffing the executive agencies which would administer the nation's business. But they counterbalanced this power by lodging in the Senate the right to approve or disapprove his key appointees and in the House of Representatives the right to initiate appropriation of the funds needed to run the government.

They made the president (of course, acting through an agent) the prosecutor of offenses against the government. But they specified that adjudication of the charges would be handled through an independent judiciary.

When to all this was added the power of impeachment (carefully structured so it could not be managed in a frivolous fashion), it would appear that the founding fathers had performed a superb job of employing reason to devise safeguards for freedom. What they had not reckoned with was the ability of the "manager" to make commitments which could not easily be revoked.

The clearest example in our history was presented by Theodore Roosevelt, who in 1907 wanted to send America's navy around the world on a "goodwill" tour. The proposal engendered a considerable amount of heat. Roosevelt's propensity for extravagant and somewhat overly masculine language had aroused fears as to his intentions. It was felt that he was uncomfortably enamored of foreign adventures and might be preparing to annex foreign territory in accordance with the traditions already established by the great imperialistic powers of Western Europe. The debate raged in Congress. Roosevelt could not send the navy (then known as the "Great White Fleet") completely around the world because he did not have the necessary money. Unfortunately for the opposition, the president did have enough funds to send the navy halfway around the world. He did so. Congress suddenly, and without warning, found itself confronted not with the choice of sending or not sending the navy but with the choice of leaving it somewhere in Asia or bringing it home. There were loud cries of "arrogance" and "bully-boy tactics." But they were futile cries and the opposition knew it. Congress dutifully voted the necessary funds and the Great White Fleet completed its round-the-world tour. The influence of this trip on America's position in world affairs may have been questionable, but its influence on Roosevelt's position domestically was clear. He was a hero simply because he had been able to act decisively, and it is a good general rule that people prefer decisive leaders. The most that Congress could do was to grumble—and grumbling has yet to win a single election.

Theodore Roosevelt, of course, was not the first president to use the power of the initiative to extend the scope of the office far beyond anything that was conceivable by the founding fathers. From the very beginning of the republic, presidents have found that it is a relatively simple matter to place Congress in a position where it has no alternative other than to back the president. This was the case in the punitive expeditions against the Barbary pirates; in the Louisiana Purchase; in the Indian wars in southern Georgia and Florida; and, more recently, in the landing of troops in the Dominican Republic and the escalation of the undeclared war in Vietnam. The president has the capacity to order troops into any area of the world, and as long as the troops are loyal, the orders will be obeyed. And once Americans are placed in a position of difficulty or peril by such orders, Congress has no alternative other than to bail them out.

Congress has no authority to issue orders other than in the discipline of its own members or in the summoning of witnesses for investigation. Consequently, its power of initiative is limited and largely negative. Interestingly enough, the Supreme Court has a form of initiative similarly negative. It can always declare the courts unable or unwilling to enforce or sanction certain laws or certain decrees and thereby render powerless other agencies of government, subsidiary forms of government, or even the common law. One of the most telling blows that the Supreme Court has struck for civil rights throughout its entire history has been its decision that racial covenants on property cannot be enforced in the courts, thereby, for all practical purposes, rendering them null and void.

The president's power of initiative, of course, is subject to certain checks. But in the field of foreign affairs and defense, these checks are almost entirely in the nature of a review. Theoretically, Congress can always hamper his activities by refusing to grant the necessary appropriations to pay for the acts taken by the executive. It is inconceivable though that Congress would refuse appropriations to support men who are fighting in the name of their country's freedom. It is also inconceivable that Congress would withhold appropriations that are essential to sustain the nation's prestige. And it is even more inconceivable that Congress would fail to approve a president's action against an avowed enemy.

The war in Vietnam has rested for years on the Gulf of Tonkin resolution, which gave carte blanche to President Johnson to take virtually unprecedented steps in Southeast Asia. Some senators have since stated that had they known what was to follow, they would not have voted for it. This, of course, is not only hindsight but nonsense. The resolution was passed following an effort to torpedo an American naval vessel in the Gulf of Tonkin and after strong U.S. air retaliation against North Vietnamese torpedo boats in Haiphong. It is unthinkable that very many members of Congress would have been willing under such circumstances to tell the world that the United States would not support its leader in a moment of national peril (actually, only two senators took that course).

In domestic affairs, however, the president's power of initiative is far less effective. This is simply because there are very few domestic crises which require an immediate affirmation of national unity. In the domestic field, Congress is willing to repudiate a president because this is something that rests within the family. It does not assume that catastrophe will follow clear evidence of division. Even here, presidents have developed techniques which give them an initiative over the legislative branch of the government. These include preparation of the budget, at which Congress can only nitpick; the establishment of revolving funds, which go a long way toward negating the appropriation authority; and the use of executive orders which have limited force of law but which can completely bypass Congress.

A most dramatic example of the latter was the executive order by which President Kennedy set up an Equal Employment Opportunity Commission that had far more drastic authority to enforce nondiscrimination than could possibly have been accorded to a legally established Fair Employment Practices Commission. This was done by the simple device of permitting the commission to cancel any government contracts if the contractor was held guilty of bigotry in his hiring practices. Congress has no adequate countermeasures to such an act. It can only react, and while the reaction can be violent, that is not equivalent to having the edge that comes with the initiative.

Almost, but not quite, as important as the power of the initiative is the ability of the chief executive to place his views before the public. This is one arena in which he has no equal from the standpoint of opportunity. When he has a point of view, that point of view can be communicated instantly to the American people, and it has behind it all the power of the nation speaking through the voice of one individual. Furthermore, the president has the capability of shaping his words as he wants them without the necessity of sifting them through a "committee" process, which hampers any similar expression of views on the part of the Congress or the courts.

The president's ability to place his views before the public is important primarily because he can usually set the terms of the national debate—and anyone who can set

the terms of a debate can win it. An outstanding example
was the manner in which Harry S Truman converted certain defeat into unexpected victory in 1948.

At the beginning of the year, no one conceded Mr.
Truman any chance for re-election. He had been plagued
by deep divisions within the Democratic party and by the
strains placed upon the economy by the postwar readjust-
ment. In 1946 the voters had signaled their disapproval by
the election of the first Republican Congress in fourteen
years, and there was no reason to believe that they were
dissatisfied with their decision. The situation was so
serious that leading Democrats debated the almost un-
heard-of possibility of denying renomination to Mr. Truman. Important leaders of the party had even proposed
that General Eisenhower be asked to be the Democratic
standard bearer (at that time no one had any idea of
General Eisenhower's politics). The Democratic convention in Philadelphia was dispirited and lackluster, with
the only heartening note a remarkable speech by Senator
Alben W. Barkley, of Kentucky—a speech which secured
for him the vice-presidential nomination. There was, of
course, no real alternative to Mr. Truman's renomination
and the delegates went along reluctantly.

But Mr. Truman was a fighter. He startled the convention and the country by declaring immediate war on
the "do-nothing, good-for-nothing, Republican-controlled,
Eightieth Congress." He whistle-stopped the nation, lam-
basting the Republican Congress at every crossroads and
every train station. The issue became the Congress itself,
and the Republican candidate, who considered his victory a foregone conclusion, made the mistake of not rallying to its defense. The outcome was Mr. Truman's election, a result so unexpected that one American newspaper

found itself on the stands with a banner headline ("Dewey Wins Election") which had been set in advance and released before the results were in. Mr. Truman had taken advantage of an important power of the presidency and had proved its effectiveness.

It must be stressed, however, that this power does not always operate with full efficacy. There are occasions when a president's voice can be subordinated to the voices of others—and Mr. Truman, paradoxically, again provides the best example. These are occasions of great danger to the American people because they usually occur when society is subject to heavy strains and authority is on the verge of breaking down. The most recent such moment in our history was the return of General Douglas MacArthur from Japan after he had been removed from his command by President Truman.

This was an instance in which a well-known rule of communications was demonstrated in its clearest form. Mechanical means of amplifying the voice and a command over all of the media are of no avail if the audience will not listen. At this crucial moment in American history, President Truman had just as many public-relations resources at his disposal as any other president up to that time. The radio networks and the then relatively feeble TV networks were his at any time he chose. Newspapers would accord him as much space as they could make available. But the American people did not want to listen.

The president had lost the most vital of all the elements in presidential authority—public confidence. It had gradually eroded under a series of political mistakes which Harry S Truman, as a senator, would never have made. A series of petty scandals—none of them of any magnitude and none of them involving the personal integrity of this unusually upright man—had made him look small and tinged with a murky variety of partisanship. Statements which he had made in defense of victims of the congressional Red scare had been so poorly phrased that he appeared to be defending Communists and communism. And he had not been able to explain the highly subtle concept of the Korean War—a war in which the objective was not victory but merely the containment of aggression.

In this turbulent context, General MacArthur appeared as a white knight in shining armor. His orotund, rolling phrases were fuzzy in meaning, but they resounded with a grandiloquence that stirred the blood of a people who wanted to feel nobility of purpose in life. His bearing was that of a haughty, aloof aristocrat, the antithesis of the American democratic ideal, but his freshly pressed uniforms were obviously unspattered by the muck of ward politics. He was greeted with an evangelical fervor which, in retrospect, is difficult to credit by those who were not actually present in the worshipping throngs that greeted his thundering procession through the United States. When he spoke, people shouted and cheered as though they were hearing the words of John the Baptist. And when, at the conclusion of an address to Congress, he recited the words of a mawkish barracks-room ballad, "Old soldiers never die, they simply fade away," men and women sobbed as though they were listening to a sermon straight from the Mount.

The administration was silent. It was absolutely helpless to dampen the ecstasy and the fervor. It feared, not without justification, that a demand by MacArthur for the reins of government would be received with a roaring "yes" from tens of millions of American throats. The situation was desperate. MacArthur was insisting on military action that could easily touch off World War III. The people were in no mood to listen to explanations. The situation was saved only by the heroic efforts of politically wise senators who ordered an investigation into the whole MacArthur episode, and chose to head it the master political craftsman of the twentieth century, Richard B. Russell, of Georgia. Russell, whose unusual mind combined the political craftiness of a nineteenth-century Tammany leader with the culture and breadth of an Oxford don, perceived the only possible solution. That was to let General MacArthur talk himself out before a congressional committee and then launch weeks of "high-level" hearings in which all the technical aspects of Asian military policy could be discussed in a classroom fashion. The hearings ended with advocates of all points of view congratulating Senator Russell for his objectivity and fairness and with MacArthur "fading away"—this time genuinely so—into obscurity. A year later, when the general addressed the Republican national convention, a reporter for a major newspaper chain noted only that he did not look so grand in civilian clothing and that the klieg lights shining on his head revealed bald spots which were not discernible in the days of his military glory. He had been forgotten but only because the arena of debate had been moved into the back room where the steam could be released gradually.

An observer, however, would be hard pressed to think of a comparable situation since the rise of electronic media of communications. Democratic strategists will never forget the powerful impact of President Eisenhower's TV speeches on the Farm Bill in 1954 and the Landrum-Griffin Act of 1958, the details of which are no longer of general interest, but which were major partisan issues at the time. In thirty minutes the careful work of months was undone, and in the latter case an overwhelming Democratic congressional majority found itself helpless to stem a popular storm. The president had triumphed in areas of economic and social legislation where his qualifications to speak were almost nonexistent. In both cases, his logic was questionable. But it did not matter. No amount of political skill could offset the president's capacity to appeal to the nation at a time when the nation had confidence in him.

The third source of presidential power is basically the ability to place others in a position of authority or prestige. This is something more than the power of appointment. A lawyer who is known to dine privately with the president (for example, Clark Clifford before he became secretary of defense) is raised to a position of eminence in the legal profession. An author who is known to be favored by the president or his family (for example, Truman Capote) finds that his readership increases overnight. A businessman who is seen at the president's elbow on more than one occasion (for example, banker Arthur Krim) finds his place in the business community enhanced. And all three are quite likely to use their newfound prestige to promote the cause of the president. By careful manipulation of such favors, a president can establish a network of Americans from coast to coast ready and anxious at any hour of the day or night to explain his cause, form supporting committees, or raise the money without which politics would be impossible. It may well be that an early sign in the decline of presidential power is the decline in the caliber of the people immediately around him.

All these powers added together are truly formidable. It is unlikely that any president could be defeated for re-election if he exercised them wisely. Franklin D. Roosevelt secured four terms in office, and it is not adequate to explain his dominance solely on the fact that he was a wartime president. Basically, he was a man who maintained his grip on reality and knew how to recover quickly from such mistakes as the Supreme Court packing bill. A president who suffers a defeat or a loss does so because he has made the wrong decisions and has not acted to recover from his errors.

The trend is clear. Over the passage of the years, what was little more than managerial authority has become power over the life of the nation itself. The right to check this power still rests in Congress and the courts. But the ability to check assumes the capacity to offer alternatives, to explain them to the public, and to manage a structure that carries them out. In the modern age, when action with little time for reflection becomes increasingly urgent, these capabilities are lessened with each passing day for every arm of the government except the presidency.

★

IV | THE MONOPOLY OF
AUTHORITATIVE ANSWERS

The essence of presidential leadership is the mechanism by which the chief executive has a monopoly on authoritative answers to crucial questions in a context of uncertainty. A president who defends and exploits his monopoly successfully is generally classified by historians as "strong." A president who permits this monopoly to be breached and allows others to dictate his response to important events is usually classified as "weak." Actually, most presidents represent a mixture of the two qualities.

Maintaining a monopoly of authoritative answers is, of course, the essence of leadership in any field. But the president has some unusual advantages which accrue to no other man. Some of these advantages flow from stated responsibilities that are clear, definite, and precise and recur year after year—such as the State of the Union message and the presentation of the budget, which set the stage for both political and governmental activity for the year. Others flow from the fact that he is the only man who has managerial control over the instruments with which a nation must respond to the crucial issues of life and death—the diplomatic services, the armed forces, the treasury, Federal public works, police agencies, etc. Were all these instrumentalities to be exploited with proper skill, it is doubtful whether any president could be removed from office except through death or senility. In actual practice, however, no president has sufficient wisdom or vitality to come up always with the proper answer, at the proper time and in the proper place. It should be noted that Franklin Roosevelt's capacity to recover from his mistakes was not shared by many of his successors or predecessors. Sooner or later, every president either responds incorrectly or fails to respond at all, and it is probable that failure to respond at all is even more deadly to the leadership of a president than failure to respond correctly.

The exercise of leadership has little or nothing to do with the personal popularity of a president. Among the responses that a president should seek to invoke from the people, liking is probably the least important. (I am not, of course, referring to the president's psychological comfort but only to his capacity to lead.) Probably no president has ever been more beloved by the American people than Dwight D. Eisenhower. He entered office on a tidal wave of enthusiasm.

His image was that of a father, a grandfather, and a kindly uncle all combined. He could do no wrong—so much so that even the revelation of a rather noisome scandal involving his closest personal adviser did not shake the public esteem for him in the slightest. And yet no man since Warren Gamaliel Harding permitted the powers of leadership to be taken from him on so many occasions.

It is instructive to examine one of the most striking instances, one that illustrates how a president can lose his power to control events almost completely even though he does not sink in personal popularity. On October 4, 1957, the Soviet Union launched into outer space the first man-made satellite, Sputnik I. The announcement of the successful venture hit the people of the United States like a brick through a plate-glass window, shattering into tiny slivers the American illusion of technical superiority over the Soviet Union and creating fears and apprehensions greater even than those which had been produced by the armed might of the Axis powers. These apprehensions reached almost a fever pitch when less than a month later—November 3, 1957—a second Sputnik was successfully placed in orbit, this time carrying a live dog as a passenger. It was obviously only a question of time until space vessels orbiting the earth would carry men far beyond the range of any conventional antiaircraft weapons. Americans · found themselves confronted with the deadliest of all fears—fear of helplessness before the unknown.

The event had not been entirely unheralded. A few years earlier, President Eisenhower had announced at a press conference that this country was starting a project to place a man-made satellite in orbit around the earth. The announcement attracted little more than passing attention. It had been explained that the satellite would be only about the size of a basketball and that its purpose would be scientific research. To a generation largely untrained in the laws of physics (and this is a safe generalization about the post-World War II generation) it was little more than a curiosity, a scientific stunt that seemed like an anticlimax following the atomic and hydrogen bombs.

The actual presence of a Soviet satellite orbiting overhead was a different matter altogether. To the feverish imagination of people too unskilled to realize the limitations of technology, it opened up limitless vistas of hideous nightmares. It was assumed that in a short time the satellites could become space stations from which atomic bombs could be dropped on the United States without any prospects of defense. Visions were created of Soviet spies with superpowerful binoculars who could ferret out the most cherished secrets of our country. Without knowing how it could be done, the "man on the street" assumed that control of the space around the earth would mean control of the earth itself. And if there was one thing of which Americans were certain in the fall of 1957, it was that they did not want the earth controlled by the Soviet Union.

The discussion and the debate, unfortunately, took place at parties, at social gatherings, in bars, in private clubs. It quickly became apparent that the administration was content to let it stay at that level. From the White House emerged only a few soothing words intimating that Sputnik and Muttnik, as they were popularly known, were merely scientific toys. President Eisenhower and his advisers were absorbed in balancing the budget and had no stomach for launching an outer-space program that obviously would cost billions of dollars and throw out the window the concepts of fiscal soundness so dear to the hearts of the "strong men" in the government— Secretary of Treasury George Humphrey and Presidential Assistant Sherman Adams. In their desire to keep things on an even keel, they neglected the most powerful instrument available to channel public discussion into rational forms—the presidential monopoly of authoritative answers.

It did not take long for another political figure to perceive the breach and rush in with political troops to seize and occupy a strong position. The Senate Democratic leader, Lyndon Johnson, had a platform from which he could operate—the Senate Armed Services Preparedness

Subcommittee. It wasn't a very potent platform in comparison to the White House. But the White House platform wasn't being used at all, and by the time the administration strategists became aware of what was happening to them, it was too late. Johnson had seized control of America's share of outer space and appeared to have elevated himself to the role of the chief—in fact the only —antagonist to Soviet domination of outer-space science.

The Senate Armed Services Preparedness Subcommittee had been little more than a caretaker operation since Johnson, its first chairman, had relinquished control of it to Senator Styles Bridges following the Republican election triumph of 1952. He had resumed the chairmanship in 1955 in addition to his majority leadership, but his preoccupation with running the Senate left him with little time to attend to its operation. Fundamentally, it was only a means of providing payroll for extra staff. Suddenly it was revitalized. Members of his personal staff on the Senate Democratic Policy Committee found themselves working full time on the Preparedness Subcommittee investigation of the outer-space program and Edwin L. Weisl, one of the nation's best-known lawyers, was brought down from New York to direct the inquiries. The Senate caucus room became the center of national attention as scientist after scientist appeared on the witness stand to tell the subcommittee members (and, through television, the entire nation) of the marvels of outer space. The first witness, Edward Teller, who had been the key physicist in developing the hydrogen bomb, was perfectly in tune with the thesis that control of outer space meant control of the earth itself. He ventured the hypothesis that the Sputnik was the first step in a process which ultimately would mean control of the weather and would place in the hands of one nation the ability to deny rainfall to another nation and turn the latter into a barren desert. Other scientists were somewhat more cautious. A few even suggested something that sounded in the time and circumstances like heresy—that exploration of the ocean depths was more important than outer space. The cautionary notes were little heeded. The American people wanted authoritative answers and if they did not come from their president, they were going to take them from the only people who offered them—Lyndon B. Johnson and the members and staff of the Senate Preparedness Subcommittee.

The administration further weakened its position by inept efforts to pooh-pooh the subcommittee's inquiry. Sherman Adams allegedly referred to the investigation as "outer-space basketball." Word leaked from the White House that President Eisenhower had remarked to some friends, "Let Lyndon Johnson keep his head in the clouds. I am going to keep my feet on the ground." These observations ran so contrary to the mood of the American people that, to the extent they were noticed at all, they were merely offensive to a slight degree. The picture was that of a president ignoring what many people regarded as the greatest crisis in centuries while the Senate Democratic leader was working night and day to mobilize the nation to meet the challenge.

The hearings brought into full public view what had previously been only hinted at by columnists, the backstage discussion on the feasibility of the intercontinental ballistic missile which allegedly could hurl atomic bombs at the United States from the Soviet Union with the speed of a rifle bullet. In retrospect it is difficult, even for people who participated in the subcommittee inquiry, to be certain of some of the conclusions that were then drawn in good faith and with a sense of absolute certainty. But it was clear that Russia had leapfrogged the United States in the development of rocketry and therefore it was assumed that the Soviets were superior in the field of ICBMs. After five years of a Republican administration, there was little doubt as to the doorstep upon which the blame would be laid.

The situation reached a climax in January, 1958, when Lyndon Johnson, in addressing the routine Senate Democratic caucus which is held at the beginning of every session, delivered a speech of compelling power. It was widely described as the "Lyndon Johnson State of the Union Address." It is now apparent that the speech was extravagant and that it overstated the situation confronting the American people. It was criticized by some Democrats (especially Mrs. Franklin D. Roosevelt) for its belligerent, somewhat martial, tone. President Eisenhower reacted, with some justification, as though an act of *lèse majesté* had been committed. But these reactions had little impact (although a few days later Johnson counterposed to the criticisms a suggestion that the development of outer-space exploration proceed under the aegis of the United Nations). The speech fitted into the public mood. The American people felt that their pride had been injured and their security threatened by the unprecedented Soviet triumph. They were willing to listen to a man who told them that they faced perils and had to react vigorously to salvage national prestige. The Space Act which followed was almost totally the work of Lyndon B. Johnson and his staff—one of the few examples in the last forty years of a major statute originating on Capitol Hill rather than in the White House. President Eisenhower succeeded only in securing the adoption of a few minor amendments.

The picture of vigorous action on the part of the Democratic congressional leadership, as contrasted to inaction on the part of the Republican executive, unquestionably played a major role in the Democratic triumphs at the polls in the fall of 1958. The contrast was highlighted by a similar reaction to the recession of 1958, when Lyndon Johnson successfully urged highway, public works, and housing programs to create employment and tugged along in his wake a reluctant President Eisenhower.

Between the two men, there was no doubt as to which was the more popular. It was President Eisenhower. Nor was there any doubt as to who, for the time being, appeared to be leading the country. It was Lyndon Johnson. The presidential powers had been usurped, to some degree, without any violation whatsoever of the Constitution and the laws. President Eisenhower had made one fatal mistake. He had not protected what should be the presidential monopoly on authoritative answers to crucial questions in a context of uncertainty. His personal popularity had not been harmed in the slightest, and within a few years the Johnson role in outer-space development was all but forgotten. Eisenhower's ability to govern had, however, been severely damaged and was not recovered until 1959 when, aroused by the Democratic electoral triumphs, he began exercising the powers of the presidency—especially through the veto. The Democratic leadership of Congress then found itself less able to dominate the national scene, even though its legislative majorities that year were larger.

The Democratic triumph in originating and enacting an outer-space statute was, of course, highly unusual. It was not repeated, except to a lesser degree in the antirecession legislation of 1958. Nevertheless, throughout the eight years of the Eisenhower administration, it was clear—even during the two years the Republicans had a majority in the House and Senate—that in political expertise the Democratic leadership of Congress had the upper hand.

To those of us who had some association with the "loyal opposition," the ease with which the Republican administration could be outmaneuvered was astonishing. There were, naturally, certain limitations to what could be done. For example, we had to start with bills sent to Congress by the president (except for the instance of outer space). But once the bills arrived, it was only a matter of time until they were overhauled and converted into laws which clearly bore the label "Democratic"—and which then usually secured a presidential blessing. Public housing was not only preserved but enhanced. Appropriations for health research were doubled and even tripled with monotonous consistency. Social security was expanded against the heated opposition of the White House. Antimonopoly amendments were written into legislation to provide for commercial development of atomic energy. In eight years, only two clear-cut victories of magnitude were won by the Republicans when the battle was clearly joined. One was the adoption of flexible farm price supports; the other was the passage of the Landrum-Griffin labor bill.

The formula was simple. It involved a careful analysis of the divisions within the two parties; a calculation of the most extreme Democratic objective that could be achieved on the basis of those divisions; the drafting of amendments calculated to unite the Democrats and divide the Republicans; and an obstinate refusal to fight for unattainable objectives. There were forces at work in the Senate and the

House that made these tactics highly successful. President Eisenhower could not afford head-on collisions with the Democratic legislators because he had to count upon their support to achieve his foreign-policy objectives, most of which were unpalatable to many members of his own party. Southern Democrats, who normally could be expected to vote with the Republicans, were more amenable to supporting the Texas leadership of Lyndon Johnson and Sam Rayburn—particularly as the belief grew in their ranks that a successful Johnson bid for the presidency was within the realm of possibility. Finally, the Republican leadership of both houses consisted of men who had played prominent roles in the anti-Eisenhower wing of their party and, though they were men of integrity, their hearts were simply not dedicated to crusading for their president.

The Democratic legislative triumphs were impressive indeed, but they are now largely forgotten and, in retrospect, this is understandable. The one thing that the Democratic leadership, for all its unquestioned superiority in political tactics, could not do was to make a serious dent in the prestige of Dwight D. Eisenhower. He concluded his second term as beloved by the American people as he had been on inauguration day. And the Democrats promptly proceeded to nominate as their candidate to be his successor John F. Kennedy, a senator who had played virtually no legislative role other than to supply a vote for the string of victories.

The forces that led to the Kennedy presidential nomination over Johnson are too complex and too irrelevant to this book to be discussed here. But the forces that sustained the high popularity of a president who was inept politically by every test except success at the polls, are very much to the point. The popularity cannot be doubted. Only once in his eight years did President Eisenhower fall below the 50 percent mark to 49 percent in April, 1958, in the midst of widespread unemployment and following his loss of leadership on the outer-space issue. Four months later the same poll showed him at 58 percent and when he left office in January, 1961, he was at 59 percent. And no practical politician doubts for a moment that the only barrier to a third term, had he so desired, was the constitutional two-term limitation imposed, ironically, by the Republican-controlled Eightieth Congress.

It is risky to speculate on the mood of a nation under any circumstances, but there are certain characteristics of the Eisenhower regime which may suggest an answer. The most important is that no man who has held the office since George Washington was better equipped to fill the role of the president as chief of state than Dwight David Eisenhower. He had dignity. He had warmth. He was obviously a man of goodwill. He sincerely believed in the validity of America's symbols and he had an almost touching faith in the capacity of "right reasoning" to solve even the most complex problems. His lack of political expertise represented the traditional American concept of politics as a grubby business in which he was uninterested, rather than a lack of intelligence. All in all, it would be difficult to find a better man to preside over a nation. He was a king without arrogance; a potentate with a distaste for power; a moralist with no touch of fanaticism. The American people could regard him with a respect and affection that they did not accord even to Franklin D. Roosevelt, who had led them out of the depression wilderness and through the largest war in recorded history. Nobody could really hate

Eisenhower (although Democratic partisans and right-wing hysterics tried) but they could, and did, hate Roosevelt. The basic difference was probably FDR's expertise which enabled him to rub salt into the wounds of his opponents time after time—an opportunity he did not forgo.

As a constitutional monarch, or a president under a parliamentary system, Ike could have had a lifetime job. And, in fact, Eisenhower's organizational methods bore some resemblance to constitutional monarchy. He himself, by all accounts, paid little attention to the day-to-day details of government. This was the business of men like George Humphrey, John Foster Dulles, Charles Wilson, Sherman Adams, and Jim Haggerty. He insisted that problems be resolved within the government itself and that the few that could not be winnowed out at lower levels be brought to him as one-page memorandums to which he could say "yes" or "no." When he made a speech, it was obviously a "speech from the throne" representing the views of "the government" rather than "the president."

To Democratic partisans, this whole process was little short of incomprehensible. We could not understand a man in a position of power who would not use the instruments of power available to him. The Democratic opposition was clever, sophisticated, and clear-eyed as to its goals, but it failed to take into account the folk wisdom which frequently rejects cleverness as trickery and political expertise as insincerity. One of the great tragedies of the Democratic party is that eight years later it still has not mastered this lesson.

In Dwight D. Eisenhower, the American people found an answer to their deep yearning for a presiding officer over their affairs. They did not care about his lack of expertise because they recognized instinctively that expertise can always be hired. They were looking for a symbol of legitimacy, continuity, and morality; and perhaps they were right in elevating these qualities to a position higher than the manipulative skill that resolves problems.

★

V | POLITICAL INFLEXIBILITY

From the standpoint of America's political structure, the major problem of the presidential system is that it can force the electorate to make a choice at a time when neither the people nor the candidates are adequately prepared. Conclusive decisions can be, and frequently are, compelled at the wrong time and under the wrong circumstances.

This situation arises out of the rhythmical character of the election machinery which has evolved. Every four years the American people are required to make a basic decision as to the continuing nature of the administrative machinery which operates the nation's affairs. Around this simple fact, a number of assumptions have arisen which determine the behavior patterns of both the electorate and the candidates. The electorate operates on the basis that frustrations with the inevitable shortcomings of any administration can find their expression only at the end of the four-year interval. Therefore, the presidential campaign takes on an air of frenetic and exaggerated passion which almost invariably results in a screaming match. Every foreign observer of the American scene has been startled by the intensity of the emotions that come to the surface and frequently appear to have little or no relevance to the campaign issues. From the standpoint of the candidate, the assumption is that the presidency is the climactic event in the life of an American politician and that he must base his whole career upon one well-organized grab at the brass ring (an assumption contrary to the experience of Grover Cleveland, William Jennings Bryan, Thomas E. Dewey, and Richard M. Nixon). He knows that a successful race depends upon the slow and careful building of a nationwide organization; upon the skillful exploitation of political issues into a solid and well-known public record; upon careful design and sculpturing of "images" so that a man can be brought before the public in clearest and sharpest focus at the ecstatic moment. All the factors must come together at the "right"—and anticipated—time.

The assumptions are complicated by the "two-term" psychology which has impressed itself so deeply on the consciousness of the American people. There arose a widespread, popular impression that presidents generally serve two terms. This concept is so deeply ingrained that it was finally written into the Constitution, under the impression that it was a "norm," by the Republican Eightieth Congress in 1947, which believed (because of Franklin D. Roosevelt's four-term stretch) that a limitation must be set to keep the presidency from being a lifetime job. The Republican leadership of the Eightieth Congress lived to regret this constitutional amendment when it prevented Dwight D. Eisenhower from running for a third term, which he obviously could have won with ease. There is no implication here that General Eisenhower *desired* a third term; merely that Republican party stalwarts regretted the fact that he could not have run for it even had he wished to do so. Had they examined their history a bit more carefully, they would have had far less concern. In this century, the concept of an eight-year rhythm has become virtually a myth.

Only once in the past forty years has there been a situation in which a president has served out two full terms and then retired in what is assumed to be the "normal" manner. That was in 1960, when President Eisenhower left the office. In this instance, the presumed rhythm of American politics worked. The candidates of the two major parties were men who had laid careful, long-range plans to drive for the presidency at the predictable time—Senator John F. Kennedy, who had begun his campaign in 1956 and Vice-President Richard M. Nixon, who had begun his campaign in 1952.

In both 1964 and 1968, however, the so-called normal rules were completely shattered and men found themselves launched into a frantic campaign for the nomination at times when they were not prepared. Both parties suffered, although the damage to the Democratic party in 1964 was not immediately apparent.

The 1964 campaign resulted in a near disaster for the Republican party, and it is a tribute to the resiliency of American political institutions that the GOP was able to recover and mount a viable presidential bid four years later. It was obvious in 1964 that the Democratic party had the election locked up tightly months in advance of the actual voting. Therefore, leading elements in the Republican establishment were not disposed to fight vigorously for the nomination. Some probably thought it was a good year to dispose of a long-standing problem—the right wing.

The right-wing political movements of the mid-twentieth century represent some of the most interesting forces in American life. In many respects, these movements are mirror images of their counterparts on the political left. And, as mirror images, they resemble the left-wing groups in those respects. As a general rule, the right-wing groups refer to themselves as "conservatives." But if the term "conservative" is defined as resistance to change and a desire to proceed along traditional lines, the right-wing use of the term is clearly a misnomer. The right-wing groups clearly desire radical—almost revolutionary—change. They seek to alter the "balance-of-power" concepts that dominate the American government on the premise that the world is in the grip of a left-wing conspiracy that can be broken only by ignoring constitutional freedoms and applying repressive measures to dissidents. Nevertheless, as these groups regard themselves as "conservative," they have tended to gather under the banner of the Republican party—frequently to the great embarrassment of Republican party leaders. They cannot be repudiated, any more than the Democratic party can repudiate its left-wing elements, simply because they provide large categories of party workers and enormous reservoirs of enthusiasm. Furthermore, there is in the American political structure no litmus-paper test for ideological purity which can determine who is truly a "Republican" and who is truly a "Democrat."

For many years, the right-wing elements in the Republican party had contended that there were vast hordes of people throughout the nation who stayed home on Election Day because there was no "conservative" candidate to attract their allegiance. It was a claim that could not be disproved. Sensible Republican leaders were unwilling to risk running a "truly conservative" candidate if there was any likelihood whatsoever that the party could win the election with a standard bearer known to be "moderate."

There were, however, some Republican leaders who felt that one experience would reveal the hollowness of the conservative claim, and that 1964 appeared to be a good year to put this concept to the test. It was obvious that Lyndon B. Johnson had captured the almost total allegiance of the American people by the masterful way in which he had taken over the reins of the government following the assassination of John F. Kennedy. Every indicator underscored the thesis that it would be a "wasted" year in the Republican calendar and consequently a good year in which to run a candidate whose defeat would not cause any widespread mourning within the GOP ranks. Barry Goldwater was nominated easily, with only a flurry of last-minute opposition from a few Republican leaders who felt that the party image was being irreparably harmed by the almost lunatic "conservative" groups that took over their convention in San Francisco.

The predictable result was one of the worst debacles suffered by any political party in American history. The Goldwater leadership was not only ideologically out of step with the American people, but also incredibly inept —a group of men with no concept whatsoever of American political life and with an absolute disdain for anyone who would make an effort to come to grips with the realities. The Republican party carried only Goldwater's home state of Arizona (by a paper-thin margin) and a few Southern states where racial issues overrode all other considerations.

The damage to the Democratic party was more subtle. In fact, as Democratic leaders jubilantly surveyed their sweeping victory, it appeared as an unalloyed triumph. There was no cloud on the horizon (even as big as a man's hand) to indicate that trouble was ahead. The trouble, of course, was created by the euphoria which resulted from victory. President Johnson and most of his close advisers interpreted the election result as a mandate from the people not only to carry on the policies of the Johnson administration but any other policies that might come to mind. There were very few voices raised at the time to warn the president that a sizable share of his victory had come from people who were literally frightened into the Democratic camp by the grotesque and preposterous campaign tactics of the opposition. The Democratic administration assumed that it was in step with the American people and proceeded accordingly without a backward look or any probing below the surface.

The victory against Senator Goldwater was also disastrous insofar as it confirmed Lyndon Johnson in his long-standing belief that party organization played a very minor role in the political life of the nation. He had developed strong resentments against the Democratic National Committee during the Eisenhower years, when the committee had served as a focal point for the forces supporting Adlai Stevenson against the Democratic congressional leadership. This resentment was nurtured over the years by the influx of the more sectarian "liberals" into party headquarters. It reached its climax in 1960 when, in his half-hearted effort to secure the presidential nomination, he found most state organizations to be under the control of John F. Kennedy.

As president, he began moving almost immediately to bring the Democratic National Committee under firm control. The moves were camouflaged because he left the committee under the nominal leadership of John Bailey, one of the early Kennedy advocates. But Bailey's staff was reduced to a minimum and the real power of the committee was lodged in the hands of a long-time political supporter—Clifton C. Carter of Texas. When Carter betrayed too much of an interest in building up the party organization, control very quickly slipped from his hands and was transferred directly to the White House, which had very little interest in maintaining any such type of activity. It was generally assumed that the 1968 election would follow the pattern of 1964, in which the personal campaign of the president himself would be the crucial factor and organization would be wholly unnecessary.

The unexpected abdication by President Lyndon Johnson on March 31 caught the party leaders totally unprepared. It had been assumed, despite many indications to the contrary, that the president would automatically be a candidate for re-election. Up to that point, only one Democrat of any stature—Senator Eugene McCarthy—had offered any kind of a presidential bid. Even he had stated quite candidly that he was not really trying to capture the presidency. He termed his "presidential" campaign merely a public platform from which he could discuss his opposition to the war in Vietnam.

In retrospect, it seems incredible that so few Democratic leaders were aware of the real weaknesses of the Johnson administration in the winter of 1968. The trusted advisers upon whom he had built his lifetime political career had all left, and he was surrounded by a new, totally inexperienced team. The Democratic party structure had been vitiated to a point where only the most perfunctory communications were maintained between the virtually empty offices of the National Committee in Washington and the baffled and frustrated leaders in the states. The rich outpouring of dynamic legislation which had characterized the Congresses of 1964, 1965, and 1966 had slowed to a trickle. The president had been successfully defied by the International Association of Machinists in the airline strike of 1966 when he had staked the prestige of his whole administration upon settling the dispute in the White House. Editorial criticism, not only of the president's policies but of his personality itself, had swelled to a crescendo. The "credibility gap" was no longer an issue but a factor taken for granted by most of the public. There was nationwide bewilderment over the inept handling of the riots which had burned out enormous chunks of some American cities in 1967 and which were clearly building up to another holocaust in 1968. The polls placed into statistical language a public image which sensitive political leaders knew existed anyway, an image which people in large masses felt was distasteful. At every appearance open to the general public, the president was met by large crowds of young people chanting, "Hey, hey, LBJ. How many kids have you killed today?"

Nevertheless, the majesty of the presidency was so great that few, if any, Democratic leaders were willing to challenge the man in the White House. The most ambitious of the lot—Robert F. Kennedy—had surveyed the scene and decided that it would be a wasted enterprise. Senator McCarthy, as stated previously, had taken the position that he was running with no hope whatsoever of securing the nomination but only to bring about a "dialogue." Probably the president himself did not realize that his political position was like the traditional castle built on sand as, shortly before his abdication, he called back to the White House two experienced political advisers who had served him in the past when his political star was in the ascendency.

The motives that led to his unanticipated withdrawal will probably never be known fully, although it came upon the heels of Senator McCarthy's unexpectedly large vote in the New Hampshire primary. At this point, a few people close to him had told him verbally that things were in very bad shape and that it would take heroic efforts not only to win the election but even to assure the nomination.

President Johnson's startling announcement threw the party leaders into a state resembling panic. Aside from Senator McCarthy, only two men were in any position whatsoever to make a bid—Vice-President Hubert H. Humphrey and Senator Robert F. Kennedy of New York. And the phrase "in any position" meant merely that they occupied places in the political structure which gave them a standing with large masses of voters. They were at least "known." But neither of them had presidential campaign organizations of the size and the scope ordinarily required at that stage of the game; neither of them had taken the necessary steps to bring their images into proper focus for the ecstatic moment. Both had obviously been thinking in terms of 1972 and both had been afraid that premature efforts would exhaust their strength and render them incapable of running at what they had assumed to be the predictable time. The situation was such, however, that they could not forgo the opening that was presented without ruling themselves out of future political life. A wild scramble began, with the candidates simultaneously launching campaigns and building campaign organizations from the ground up.

Senator Kennedy created enthusiasm and generated an air of excitement wherever he went, but he did not gather in the delegates. It was apparent to professional political observers, even before his assassination in Los Angeles, that his campaign was a losing cause. The excitement came from very young people and from militant sections of the black population, both of which could play a role but neither of which could be decisive in the political processes. Vice-President Humphrey, on the other hand, generated little or no excitement but gathered in the delegates with astonishing rapidity, assuring himself of a first-ballot nomination weeks before the convention. The delegates were hardly enthusiastic but they subconsciously followed a simple rule of thumb—only Humphrey could hold the party together. In the entire history of American politics no political party had succeeded in winning an election after a serious split.

The Republican party, unlike the Democrats, had one candidate who was ready. For eight years, Richard M. Nixon had been plodding the Republican fund-raising circuit—appearing at party dinners, showing up when no one else would, placing in his political debt virtually every leader throughout the United States. Other Republicans —possibly even some with more magnetic personalities— had assessed 1968 in the same light as the Democratic party leaders. They had assumed that there would be little profit in running against a Democratic president who had served only one term, and they were not excited about the prospects. Governor Romney of Michigan had mounted a campaign early in the year but took himself out because of adverse polls even before the New Hampshire primary. The president's announcement created as much shock in their ranks as it did among the Democrats. Nobody was prepared, except Nixon. There were wild flurries within the Republican ranks—an "in again, out again" movement by Governor Rockefeller of New York and an abortive, last-minute drive by Governor Reagan of California. Though the Republican rank and file were not overly enthusiastic about Nixon, his troops were too well organized. He had figured that 1968 was truly his "last main chance" year and he was ready when no one else was prepared. He was nominated at the Miami convention on the first ballot.

The significant point, however, is that in the summer of 1968 no candidate on the scene fired the American people with the kind of enthusiasm generated by Dwight D. Eisenhower in 1952 or Franklin Delano Roosevelt in 1932. This was not the fault of the candidates. It was simply that they had to plunge into the maelstrom at the wrong time, from the wrong platforms, and under the wrong circumstances. There was nowhere a ground swell powerful enough to result in the election of a president with the force of public opinion behind him that a chief executive must have at the beginning of his term—especially when he faces the extraordinary problems that now confront the United States.

The campaign of 1968 was one of the most lackluster in American history. It stood out in the public mind only because of the riots at the Chicago Democratic convention; some gaffes from the Republican vice-presidential candidate (verbal errors of no real importance); the unexpected appeal to intellectuals and young people of the Democratic vice-presidential candidate; and the high degree of enthusiasm generated for the third-party candidate—George Wallace. Third-party candidates, of course, rarely corral many votes, and at the polls the Republican and Democratic candidates split almost even—Mr. Nixon with slightly more than 43 percent and Mr. Humphrey with slightly less than 43 percent. Mr. Nixon was thus launched upon his presidency with no popular enthusiasm behind him.

In a parliamentary system, the nodal factors of American politics would be obviated. The execu-

tives of the government live in a state of continuing ac-
countability to the electorate. They know that they can be
called before the bar of public opinion through the simple device of a parliamentary vote of no confidence at any
time. Therefore it is incumbent upon them to remain in
touch with the people of the nation in full awareness that
there are limits of tolerance, and that to stray beyond those
limits means ouster from office. In addition, ouster from
office does not mean the end of a political career. The
prime minister (unless he decides voluntarily to retire)
merely becomes the leader of "the loyal opposition"—a
position in which his experience and his "feel" for the nation's problems are not lost to the country.

Even more important, the parliamentary system guar-
antees that political life will be a continuing ferment, with
constant interaction between the voters and the national
managers. The managers are subjected to daily bombard-
ments by frustrated citizenry. On the other hand, the
frustrations do not have the explosive quality that
characterize a people who only have one opportunity every
four years to affect their nation's destiny.

A parliamentary system requires a continuing exercise of the political skills which are all too often derided
by American folklore. In our modern, highly mechanized,
highly independent social structure, it would be well to
give consideration to a structure that would place a higher
value upon the humanistic aspects of the political art.

★

The cabinet is one of those institutions in which the whole is less than the sum of the parts. As individual officers, the members bear heavy responsibilities in administering the affairs of the government. As a collective body, they are about as useful as the vermiform appendix— though far more honored.

The late President Kennedy was almost openly scornful of the institution. He did not express his feelings in public statements but numerous "background" stories in the press—obviously based on direct contacts with him —made his position clear. He held very few cabinet sessions and sought instead to improvise top-level groups which would have some meaning.

In the Cuban missile crisis, for example, he not only ignored the cabinet but even broadened the National Security Council—the president, the vice-president, the secretary of state, and the secretary of defense. National policy was directed by an ad hoc "executive" committee composed of officials in whose judgment he had an unusually high degree of confidence. According to the accounts of many who were present during the deliberations, the most important was probably his brother, Attorney General Robert Kennedy.

The Kennedy thesis that the cabinet was not a useful instrument was proved to the hilt by his successor, Lyndon B. Johnson. It is doubtful whether any president in our history made more of an effort to elevate the status of the institution, and the result was totally negative. Cabinet meetings were held with considerable regularity, with fully predetermined agendas and fully prewritten statements. In general, they consisted of briefings by cabinet members followed by a later release of the statements to the press. It was regarded by all participants except the president as a painful experience, somewhat akin to sitting with the preacher in the front parlor on Sunday, and the press was quite successful in concealing its enthusiasm for the news releases that followed. It should be noted that a special assistant had the full-time job of thinking up topics for the cabinet. No governmental group in the mainstream of public life ever needs a special effort to devise reasons for meeting.

Individual members of the cabinet had great influence on the president at various times—notably Robert S. McNamara, Dean Rusk, and Stewart L. Udall. But this had nothing to do with their position in the cabinet and only slightly more to do with their status as secretaries. Essentially, it was the personal desires of the president that determined the favorite and, as Mr. McNamara learned, favor that is granted is favor that can be withdrawn.

The issue of the cabinet is of interest to this book only in the sense that it could be one instrumentality for keeping a president in contact with reality. There need be no waiting for the answer. It is not such an instrumentality and cannot be. At best, it constitutes a group of oddly assorted advisers with only a few working interests in common. The usefulness of an adviser under any circumstances depends upon the willingness of his audience to listen.

In many respects, it is unfortunate that the cabinet cannot play this role. Cabinet members tend to be men of distinction, a status which does not assure the possession of capacity and breadth of vision but which lengthens the odds that such qualities will be present. The natural desire of any political figure to broaden the base of his support leads to appointments which are always well balanced geographically and sometimes well balanced politically. Finally, the secretaries tend to have that serenity that comes from discharging specific responsibilities and that tends to make men more objective in their evaluation of a situation. By every criterion, cabinet advice should be good advice—at least, well tempered, informed, and prudent.

There is one missing ingredient. Even though a president may make political use of the members, individually and collectively, it is not a political body. A cabinet meeting may be called to cloak an important political move with an aura of respectability. Cabinet members may be sent around the country to defend a presidential policy at public opinion forums. Individual secretaries may even hit the hustings and plug for candidates during an election campaign (but never, by tradition, the secretaries of state or defense). Patronage problems may be centered officially in a cabinet member (usually the postmaster general). But these are all moves directed by the president. They do not lie in the realm of individual choice. The secretaries do not have a political status and it is considered bad form for any one of them to deviate in the slightest from the line laid down by their chief—so bad that deviation usually spells an end to a public career.

An outstanding example of such deviation in the past few decades was presented by the Iowa mystic Henry A. Wallace, a man who had remarkable appeal but who confused the American cabinet system, along with many other things, with the system of a parliamentary government. As secretary of commerce, he took strong (the word "sharp" was inappropriate for Mr. Wallace) issue with Harry S Truman. Mr. Truman was unusually tolerant about such things, but he could not have a member of his official family challenging the whole basis of his foreign policy. A parting of the ways was negotiated within hours after one of Mr. Wallace's speeches. The latter's subsequent political career was notable only for some very brief, very odd, and very dreamlike alliances that culminated in a humiliatingly unsuccessful attempt to damage Mr. Truman's prospects in the 1948 election. After that, there was only obscurity.

The interesting feature was the reaction to the Wallace speech that led to the rupture. There were a good many people who agreed with what he had to say (primarily that stronger initiatives should be taken to break the deadlock of the Cold War) but who were incensed over what they believed was disloyalty to the chief. They felt that he should have resigned from the cabinet first and established an independent political position before criticizing the president. It is difficult to judge how deeply such opinions were held among the public, as the conduct of the Progressive party, which adopted Mr. Wallace as its candidate, was hardly calculated to win widespread popular support. It was an organization more interested in gaining

converts than in picking up votes and the electorate reacted accordingly. Nevertheless, Mr. Wallace's vote was remarkably small. Many of the newsmen who covered him
thought that it did not coincide either with his personal
popularity or the acceptance of many of his concepts. It is
quite possible that the picture of apostasy he presented
was catastrophic.

The tradition of cabinet loyalty to the chief is so
strong that when members do leave, their departure is ac-
companied by a barrage of statements refuting even the
suggestion of a break with the president. These assurances
come not only from the White House but from the depart-
ing cabinet member himself. Regardless of the motivations, the final scene must be one of intense—almost
anxious—cordiality, with broad grins and handshakes carefully exaggerated so they will be missed by no camera.

This, of course, does not mean that a cabinet member will deliberately alter his views or lie to a president
about his feelings. When a president polls the group, which
happens frequently, he will receive brief, concise, carefully worded statements that will establish for the record
the secretaries' positions. This is a very useful method for
gathering advice on issues where nobody feels very
strongly and the only problem is the refinement of methods
for reaching predetermined goals. But the issues that
really matter—the issues of survival—*do* stir men's emotions and cannot be discussed meaningfully in an atmosphere reminiscent of classroom recitation.

There is no such thing as adversary discussion in a
cabinet meeting. Men do not pound the table, contradict
each other, challenge contrary opinions. Whatever fire may
have been in their bellies when they entered the White
House gate has been carefully quenched by the time

they reach the Cabinet Room doorsill. What follows is a gentlemanly discourse conducted on an extremely "high" level, and enveloped in the maximum dullness conceivable. And every word is addressed to one man and one man only. A cabinet meeting is not a marketplace of thought where ideas undergo crucial tests. It is, at best, a forum for the presentation of ideas which could just as easily— and perhaps more usefully—be gathered over the telephone or by mail.

In reality, there is nothing else that it can be. The cabinet members have no firm political base. They represent no partisan constituency, in the commonly accepted sense of that term. Their personal politics are totally irrelevant to their official position, except for the rare cases in which they are asked to do some political chores for the head man. They are servants of the president and their loyalties are legitimately to him and to *his* policies rather than to a set of principles which bind together a group of people in the population.

If they owed their public position to another political party or even to an opposition faction within the president's own party, the situation would be quite different. Then they would have a base for challenge, for expressing the kind of dissent that a president should hear on a direct, personal basis if he is to remain in touch with reality. A president may, of course, seek on occasion to placate an opposition by appointing one of its representatives to his cabinet. But this is something that he does according to the dictates of his own judgment and something he can undo by his own choosing. The opposition cannot have such an appointment by right, no matter how significant the size of its popular following.

No president would ever want a cabinet which was

anything other than harmonious. Chief executives are human and prefer "discussions" which are never sharper than suggestions on how to improve the tactics of an already determined course of action. By the time an issue reaches a level where it should be considered by men of cabinet status, this is the kind of discussion he needs the least. There should be some body of men with whom he has a working relationship who can be severe and even unpleasant in their criticisms before he takes the final plunge.

Perhaps I am unduly influenced by the many years that I spent working for the Senate. But I do not believe that a cabinet which had a built-in device for adversary relationships would be chaotic. I doubt whether it would bring the country to a standstill except possibly on issues where our people are so divided that action is impossible anyway. Of course, there would have to be some device for dissolving the cabinet when it hit a stalemate, and assembling another group of men to give it the old college try. But other countries have found such devices and they have/ worked reasonably well.

Perhaps I should revert to the reference to the Senate in the paragraph above. The hierarchs of that body are extremely strong-minded men who do not hesitate to express their opinions of each other in basic English, as long as the *Congressional Record* clerk is not around. Sometimes even the presence of the clerk affords little restraint. Yet they are able to find ways of coalescing rapidly when any real crisis presents itself, and these ways reach not only through all factions but across the center aisle. And for men so well endowed with the qualities of self-esteem, they are usually quite realistic about their problems.

This is not intended to present senators as ideal candidates for the presidency or to assert that the Senate way of doing business is a model for the executive branch. But it is to say that the Senate rarely strays any great distance from political reality and that its members have no real difficulty working together. This is a proposition that will be disputed in Washington, where the all-pervasive nature of the executive branch dominates the lives of most of the inhabitants. But I invite those who have had experience at both ends of Pennsylvania Avenue to ponder my conclusions.

Even more interesting, however, is the fact that senators do *not* play the role of adversary in the presence of the chief executive. This is not because entry into the portals of the White House taps previously unrealized reserves of diffidence. It is simply that they have found it inadvisable to be anything other than respectful. The aura of reverence that surrounds the president when he is in the Mansion is so universal that the slightest hint of criticism automatically labels a man as a colossal lout.

The wise senator, therefore, enters cautiously, dressed in his Sunday best and with a respectful, almost pious, look on his face. He waits to speak until the president has spoken to him and his responses are couched in the same careful language employed by cabinet members. He emerges in the same manner and if, for any reason, he must express a dissent, it is most deferential, almost apologetic. There have been exceptions, of course, but they often end disastrously for the senator. A good example was provided by the late William E. Borah of Idaho, who emerged from a conference with President Roosevelt snorting that his sources of information were superior to those of the White House and that he was quite confident there would be no war in Europe that year. That was just a few months before the Germans marched into Poland.

When a president's influence with the public begins to wane, the situation does change to the extent that the voices on the Senate floor become quite raucous. During an election campaign they will become abusive. But this is still something a president reads in a newspaper or views on TV. This is not of the same order as face-to-face confrontation. When the latter occurs, even the most boorish of senators becomes quite civilized. There is no such thing as a challenge to a president on his home ground.

In truth, there is no such challenge anywhere within the government. Members of the judiciary deal with a president at arm's length—a wise rule whose occasional violation invariably results in unpleasant, and sometimes disastrous, consequences. Some of the regulatory agencies include members who, by law, must be members of an opposition party, but they move in circles as remote from the White House as the judiciary—pretty much for the same reasons. The heads of the independent agencies—such as NASA—are in even less of a position to issue a challenge than their more prestigious colleagues in the cabinet. The "underground opposition" within administrative circles, which inevitably exists as a holdover from the past, can do very little other than to circulate scandalous stories, a practice quite rightly frowned upon but which will persist.

I am well aware that the concept of including opposition within the government itself will not be welcomed by any president or by many administrative officials. It seems messy and inefficient, and there is a tendency to assume that a president should not be burdened with an official family some of whose members may make him uncomfortable.

The answer to the second problem—the extra burdens that a president would have to bear—is that he must bear those burdens anyway. The success of any presidential program depends upon public support. Whatever divisions a president might have to face within the Cabinet Room are divisions he will face when his designs become public. He would be in far better shape if he were compelled to take the opposition into account at the time his proposals were being developed. It would be preferable to abandon a program when quiet discussion disclosed its inability to attain goals (unless there was an educational aspect involved) than to throw it out to the wolves and be surprised when it met defeat. The reality is, of course, that very few programs would be abandoned, but many would be modified into a far more sensible form.

It is amazing how few presidential programs reach Congress in a palatable form. The history of the past thirty-three years has been a rarely broken record of presidential swimming in hot congressional water. President Roosevelt, after the first few years when the country regarded him as a savior, was virtually unable to get the House and Senate to move on a domestic proposal. His place in history was probably saved by World War II. President Truman made a magnificent start in securing passage of vital foreign-policy legislation but spent most of his terms in a kicking, snarling match with Capitol Hill. President Eisenhower left Congress alone as much as possible but even he was saved from endless wrangling only because a subtle Democratic opposition conceived and carried out the tactic of converting his few proposals into vehicles for Democratic legislation. President Kennedy's legislative program was stalled on dead center at the time of his assassination and the only important items that ever reached the White House were a few salvaged by his successor. President Johnson, widely regarded as the genius of the Senate in the twentieth century, shoved a fantastic number of bills down congressional throats. But this was due chiefly to the fact that he, also, looked like a savior after the traumatic shock of the assassination. He ended his term in an atmosphere of rebuff after rebuff, scarcely speaking to his old friends. President Nixon in his early months in office should still have been in the glowing phase of the traditional "honeymoon." Yet he encountered serious trouble on two major proposals—extension of the income-tax surcharge and authority to construct a modified antiballistics missile system. The fact that the struggle began so early is significant.

It is not enough to blame President Truman's and President Johnson's problems on the Korean and Vietnam wars and President Eisenhower's difficulties on lack of experience. There are, in my judgment, far deeper roots to the warfare between two of our major branches of government—warfare that goes beyond the antagonisms foreseen by the founding fathers when they set up a system of divided powers. The answer is that a president does not have available to him methods of gauging the intensity of the opposition—something that any politician must have in order to be successful. He lives in an environment where it is not possible to make valid, intuitive judgments about just how angry people will become and about what must be done to blunt their opposition without losing sight of his objective.

Of course, he finds out soon enough once his proposal becomes public. The legislative liaison staff is quite efficient at determining such things once a message has hit the floor of Congress. By that time, it is too late. The president's positions are solidified. Even slight modifications then appear as an embarrassing retreat and, rather than be humiliated, the project is often dropped.

The master practitioners of the Senate seldom fall into this trap. They live in an atmosphere which will instill some degree of humility into even the most arrogant of men. They walk every day through an adversary atmosphere. They have before them constant reminders of the swift penalties for failure to take into account the strong feelings of other men. They not only receive letters and telephone calls from their constituents but run into them in the corridor daily. Reality is never very far away.

The executive branch of the government cannot, of course, operate at the leisurely pace of the Senate. A legislative body, except in highly unusual circumstances, does not have to hurry. But there should be some way that policy decisions could be made at a top level of government through adversary processes. Time would be lost in making many decisions, but when we look at the immediate past, it is difficult to avoid the thought that more time should be lost and perhaps many of the decisions never made. And a great deal of the time would be made up by moving more quickly to action.

We have become too fearful of the results of disputatious personalities and clashing ideologies. We assume that the political process is a type of warfare in which the leaders are justified in concealing their plans from friend and foe alike and awaiting the psychological moment to strip off the protective covering and open fire. We assume that such tactics lessen the damage from partisan strife. Politics *is* a form of warfare but it is designed to achieve different goals and therefore should be played under different rules. The earlier the differences are brought into the open, the better. Perhaps if we forgot some of our vaunted efficiency, we would score somewhat better in the realm of achievement.

★

VII | THE PRESSURE COOKER

A president's most persistent problem in staying in touch with reality lies in his staff. It is the aspect of White House life that bears the most striking resemblance to a court. As a rule, it is seen by outsiders in terms of the type of staff which assists a commander or a corporation executive. But this is not its true character. The man it serves is neither a military commander nor a business administrator.

The White House staff has an inner political life of its own. It consists of people who do not have fixed responsibilities—except in the rare instance of a President Eisenhower who brought to the White House the staff and command organization of the army and imposed it with relentless and unyielding determination. The mere fact, however, that President Eisenhower could do this demonstrates the basic character of the staff. It is the creature of the president, a group of men who have one purpose in life and one purpose only—to perform personal services for the man in charge.

Prior to Franklin D. Roosevelt's era, White House staffs

were small. They consisted, at most, of a few personal secretaries and aides. Occasionally, a president like Woodrow Wilson would keep close to him a trusted adviser like Colonel House. But Colonel House was not a staff aide in any real sense of the term. He was a personal friend, who stayed physically within the White House for purposes of convenience.

Since Franklin D. Roosevelt, the practice has increased of assigning titles and outlining, on paper at least, responsibilities for the members of the staff. Today, there is a press secretary; a special assistant for national security affairs; a special assistant for cabinet affairs; a special assistant for independent agencies; a special assistant for minorities; a special assistant for legislative liaison; a special counsel. But the titles have very little substance behind them. The special counsel, for example, does very little real legal work; for legal opinions the White House tends to lean upon the executive agencies, especially the Justice Department. In the last two administrations, the special counsels have been primarily speech writers (Theodore Sorensen and Harry McPherson), and while both were men of high legal competence their opinions on points of law were rarely sought or offered. It was open knowledge, not only in the White House but to the Washington community at large, that their ability to put on paper sentences that would parse grammatically was the key to their position in the hierarchy.

To some extent, of course, the titles do have meaning. In these few cases, it is only because there are some functions in the White House that require an institutionalized approach and comprise continuing responsibilities on a day-to-day basis. The special assistant for national security affairs, for example, generally does handle national security affairs. His clear-cut role rests not upon his expertise in international relations but upon the somewhat more mundane fact that he controls the flow of communications concerning them to the president. These communications are highly complex. They enter the White House in a bewildering flood. There must, of necessity, be routine procedures which pare them down to a point where they are digestible by the president. The administration of these procedures is a full-time job. Therefore, it follows that the man who holds it has the rare and cherished privilege in the White House of doing what he is supposed to do.

Another example of a position which has been institutionalized is that of the White House press secretary. But again, this is not due to the press secretary's expertise in handling the press, or, as it is more delicately termed, public relations. Public relations is actually the function of the president himself. Every president, in reality, is his own press secretary (and this is probably reflected in the nature of the relations between the press and the presidents—it is something like a man being his own lawyer). The press secretary, however, has a series of routine duties which must be attended to by a full-time assistant. They are very unglamorous duties. They consist of chartering airplanes so the press can follow the president (the press pays for the airplane, not the taxpayer); of arranging hotel accommodations; of notifying telegraph and telephone companies where extra press facilities will be needed; of arranging with police departments for special credentials for the press as the president travels about the country; of dealing with the television networks as to where cameras can be placed. Without these arrangements, there could be no adequate coverage of a president. They are sufficiently exhausting, and require a sufficient degree of continuity, that it is not possible to allocate the responsibilities among a number of assistants to be performed on an ad hoc basis. It is probable that Jim Haggerty was the only press secretary in the history of the White House who actually performed the job in accordance with the popular concept—dealing with and administering press policy. But again, he was able to do so only because he served a president who was rigidly determined to delegate every administrative detail. It is unlikely that we shall have such a president again unless the constitutional basis for electing the chief of state is altered.

For other White House assistants there is only one fixed goal in life. It is somehow to gain and maintain access to the president. This is a process which resembles nothing else known in the world except possibly the Japanese game of *go*, a contest in which there are very few fixed rules and the playing consists of laying down alternating counters in patterns that permit flexibility but seek to deny that flexibility to the opponent. The success of the player depends upon the whim of the president. Consequently, the president's psychology is studied minutely, and a working day in the White House is marked by innumerable probes to determine which routes to the Oval Room are open and which end in a blind alley.

The techniques are astonishingly simple and require not subtlety but a willingness to test human credulity to its outermost limits. Basically, the methodology is to be present either personally or by a proxy piece of paper when "good news" arrives and to be certain that someone else is present when the news is bad. The battle-wise assistant develops to its highest degree the faculty of maintaining physical proximity coupled with the ability to disappear (by ducking down a hallway or stepping behind a post) at the right moments. The White House is architecturally well adapted to such tactics, since there are plenty of hallways and a plethora of concealing pillars.

When a president is happy and pleased, his assistants race behind him shoulder to shoulder in lockstep as he strides from the West Wing to the family quarters. When storm signals are flying, because of a "bad" column or an insulting statement by a foreign leader, the president makes the journey alone, watched only by the unblinking eyes of the Secret Service and the uniformed police who guard the Mansion.

The written word is crucial. But it is important that memorandums reach the president at the "right" moment, and this is something no assistant can manage personally. There is a traditional approach, however, which never fails. The way to a man's heart may be through his stomach but the best path to his favorable attention usually lies through his secretary—especially if she is fully endowed with the age-old feminine faculty of measuring masculine emotional temperature with precision. The assistant so fortunate as to have a secretary who rooms with that secretary has won three-quarters of the battle. It is even conceivable that his suggestions will go to the top of the stack while others are rerouted without even receiving presidential attention.

The question of physical proximity in terms of office space is a primary cause of battle. The favored position in the past was the West Wing, which housed the special counsel, the national security council staff, the legislative liaison staff, the press secretary, the special assistant for cabinet affairs, and the appointments secretary. An office in the East Wing automatically relegated its possessor to the status of "resident intellectual"—someone who was useful as window dressing when academic meetings were being held but who was not to be entrusted with the important business of the nation. An assignment to the Executive Office Building was banishment to the outer darkness of the technical world, made up of people who were "useful" and well informed but who did not have the ear of the president and therefore did not participate in what is euphemistically called "making policy." Mr. Nixon has changed the geographical locations but it is a safe bet that the essential nature of the struggle for position remains unchanged.

It is vitally important to the White House assistant that he receive a constant flow of information on the moods of the president and the latest problems that are preoccupying his attention. Since the assistant himself cannot be present in more than one place at a time and since he cannot be too obvious in his search for intelligence, he himself must have an assistant—preferably one who is young, ambitious, hyperthyroid, and possessed of an excellent pair of feet. A considerable amount of the motion that characterizes the White House is due to the restless prowling of the assistants to the assistants, and a courtier is well advised not to leave his office empty with imprudent papers on his desk. If he does, he may suffer the major penalty of indiscretion—an unexpectedly sharp remark from the president or, even worse, the expounding of one of his cherished ideas by another.

The only aspect of "palace-guard" politics which requires subtlety is the use of the press. The inexperienced courtier may make the mistake of using his press contacts (which it takes a positive effort of will not to acquire) to secure favorable mention of his name in public. But the wilier practitioners of the art of palace knife-fighting take a different tack. They seek to feature their competitors' names in a context which will displease the man who holds the real power. This reverse-thrust technique is somewhat more complex than it appears on first glance. It is not inconceivable, for example, that a newspaper story speculating on the promotion of an assistant to higher office may be the death knell of that assistant's governmental career. It all depends upon the psychology of the president, but whatever that psychology, there will always be people around him who are willing to play it for whatever it is worth.

It is a stultifying business, and history prepares us poorly for the realities of palace intrigue. Somehow, in the studies of past monarchies, the intrigants loom larger than life—men and women of titanic, though evil, proportions—and the intrigues appear as fiendishly cunning, intricate, and complex plots. It comes as a shock to discover that the principals are small bore and the plots themselves dreary.

The sensitive mind boggles at the revelation that the empty-headed girl with the Betty Boop pout and the vacant stare, idly painting her fingernails alongside an IBM typewriter, is a twentieth-century Nell Gwyn, or that the neatly groomed youth with the choirboy face, spouting the liturgical clichés of the behavioral sciences, is Rasputin with a haircut. Even more shattering psychologically is the realization that the assistant who shows up at the bedchamber at 7:15 in the morning with a Gallup poll demonstrating a five-point rise in popularity is displaying the total sum of the *court* wisdom of a Richelieu (who, of course, had other forms of wisdom, as well) or that the absurdly posturing young man who is careful to present a secretary with frilly lingerie at Christmas, is following in the footsteps of Potemkin. History, in this respect, has let us down badly—not by telling us that virtue always conquers evil but by painting pedestrian activities in exciting colors.

The White House assistant must learn early that his enemy is not towering evil but boring inanity. If he is to survive, he must drop his preconceived notions and get down to the proper level. It is one thing to battle Grendel—another thing to grapple with Sammy Glick. Either can be handled by employment of the appropriate tactics. But Grendel is at least predictable—he fights in the field with club and sword. It is only Glick who appears disconcertingly at the banquet table in the castle armed with the deadlier weapons of flattery and piety. The life of a courtier is to be Sammy Glick or to fight Sammy Glick—and all of his sisters and his uncles and his cousins and his aunts. Sammy has the edge because he cares more about the prize.

The most desired position, the one that symbolizes ultimate triumph, is attendance in the morning when the president first awakens, rested and ready to transact business. To occupy this position, no sacrifice is too great. An assistant will arise at three or four in the morning and hustle down to the White House looking for an excuse to dash over to the Mansion with a memorandum. If he is successful, he can return to the West Wing with the ultimate symbol of success—the mission of relaying to the other assistants the presidential decisions and the presidential orders for the day. If he can succeed in fulfilling this function for several days in a row, he becomes known as "the most influential man in the White House" and his triumph is complete.

This title, incidentally, may be bestowed upon one person in the privacy of the Mansion and upon quite a different person in the public press. No one who has ever worked in the White House can escape a feeling of skepticism in future years when he reads accounts of the relative positions of special assistants in the hierarchy.

The problem is twofold—the reaction of the system upon the assistants themselves, and the reaction of the system upon the presidents. There is good reason to believe that it is unhealthy in either case.

It is an exhausting life but there is solace along embassy row and in the drawing rooms of Georgetown hostesses. The presidential assistant, wearied from a long day with the knife, can find ample diversion any night of the week. He may feast on couscous at the Saudi Arabian Embassy, sip champagne with the French, or plump delicate mini-tamales into his mouth among the Mexicans. He cannot do this all in one night but he can be certain there will be some action somewhere in town and he has the added advantage of not needing an invitation. Doors open automatically for him and he can step into any party to the fluttering and flattering attention of the hostess and whatever society writers have been assigned to the event. At least once in his tenure, he will dine *tête-à-tête* with the Soviet ambassador and his wife in a small room where the atmosphere is intimate and the food is served family style.

Of course, there is a penalty to be paid for these ever-beckoning delights. There are presidents who do work nights (following an afternoon's nap), and a man's position in the pecking order can easily be shifted by his presence or absence at a crucial moment when a prompt explanation may satisfy presidential curiosity or assuage presidential wrath. An assistant knows that no matter what hour he leaves the building someone will still be there with access to a presidential "hot line," even if it is only the duty officer in the situation room (referred to by adepts as the "sit" room).

A White House assistant lives a life of anxiety. There is no fixed point in his daily routine, other than the occasional smile of approbation or nod of approval that comes from the president. He is denied the inner comfort of a man who has a specific task to perform and who is measured by professional standards as to whether he has performed the task well or poorly. He may be aware of the fact that his performance on any specific assignment may be good, even superb in objective terms. But this is of no importance if there is a failure of appreciation on the part of his chief. Therefore, except for highly unusual men, the goal is not to perform superbly but to perform spectacularly. The two aims are not aways compatible.

There is, on the part of White House assistants, a tendency to bring to the White House problems which should not properly be there, frequently to the disadvantage of the president. In recent years, far too many labor disputes have been brought within the gates, where they could receive the personal attention of the president. There are times, of course, when the dispute raises issues so perilous to the health and safety of the United States that such action is justified. This can be said of the railroad strike in 1964. But there is reason to believe that neither the steel strike of 1965 nor the maritime strike of 1966 should have been so treated. Both were settled successfully but they merely paved the way for bringing into the White House the airline strike of 1966 that resulted in a disastrous setback to President Johnson. It is doubtful whether he would have taken over this dispute had he not been surrounded by assistants whose eyes were fixed on the possibility of a spectacular announcement rather than on the long-range trends in labor-management relations which made it impossible to achieve a settlement by executive intervention.

From the president's standpoint, the greatest staff problem is that of maintaining his contact with the world's reality that lies outside the White House walls. Very few have succeeded in doing so. They start their administrations fresh from the political wars, which have a tendency to keep men closely tied to the facts of life, but it is only a matter of time until the White House assistants close in like a pretorian guard. Since they are the only people a president sees on a day-to-day basis, they become to him the voice of the people. They represent the closest approximation that he has of outside contacts, and it is inevitable that he comes to regard them as humanity itself.

Even the vision of so earthy a politician as Lyndon B. Johnson became blurred as the years went by. He mistook the alert, taut, well-groomed young men around him for "American youth" and could never comprehend the origins of the long-haired, slovenly attired youngsters who hooted at him so savagely when he traveled (and eventually made most travel impossible) and who raged and stormed outside the White House gates. To him, they appeared to be extraterrestrial invaders—not only non-American but nonearthly. Certainly, they did not fit the pattern of young men and young women whom he had assembled so painstakingly and who were so obviously, in his eyes, the embodiment of the nation's dream.

The man who resisted this temptation most strongly, and who maintained his political skill longer than any other president, was Franklin D. Roosevelt. He understood thoroughly the weaknesses of the staff system in the White

House. He saw to it that under no circumstances could the people in his immediate vicinity control his access to information. Every staff assistant from the New Deal days recalls the experience of bringing a report to FDR and discovering, in the course of the conversation, that the president had gained from some mysterious, outside source knowledge of aspects of the project of which the assistant himself was not aware. No assistant, with the possible exception of Harry Hopkins, ever felt that his position was secure. And none of them would have dared to withhold any information. The penalties were too swift and too sure to permit what would anyway have been a futile exercise.

It is difficult, however, for a president to maintain sources of information outside his immediate staff. It requires a positive effort of will. This situation arises from the general nature of the presidency.

Every political leader, of course, must have assistants and close associates in whom he can repose absolute confidence. The political life is a life of struggle in which a man is surrounded by enemies who will take advantage of any show of vulnerability. Only a band of people unified in a common purpose and determined to follow their leader through fire and storm can possibly survive. But for most politicians, there are day-to-day tests of each individual member of his following. He is told—immediately and unpleasantly—whenever any of his subordinates has made a bad "fluff" or has overstepped what is generally regarded as the bounds of legitimate warfare.

For many years, a corporation sold a popular mouthwash to the American people on the basis that it would inhibit bad breath. The slogan under which the product was merchandised—"Even your best friends won't tell you"—meant that the subject was too delicate to mention and that a person could exude the foulest odors without being aware of the fact. As far as the mouthwash was concerned, the slogan was somewhat misleading—not only your best friends but your worst enemies will tell you if you have bad breath. But the concept that "even your best friends won't tell you" about unpleasant things applies with tremendous force to the president.

As noted, an essential characteristic of monarchy is untouchability. No one touches a king unless he is specifically invited to do so. No one thrusts unpleasant thoughts upon a king unless he is ordered to do so, and even then he does so at his own peril. The response to unpleasant information has been fixed by a pattern with a long history. Every courtier recalls, either literally or instinctively, what happened to the messenger who brought Peter the Great the news of the Russian defeat by Charles XII at the Battle of Narva. The courtier was strangled by decree of the czar. A modern-day monarch—at least a monarch in the White House—cannot direct the placing of a noose around a man's throat for bringing him bad news. But his frown can mean social and economic strangulation. And only a very brave or a very foolish man will suffer that frown.

Furthermore, an outsider has a sense of diffidence in approaching a president to tell him "the facts of life" about his staff. It is in the same class as telling a father about the shortcomings of his son. The only people who will do it are boors, whose opinion is little valued under the best of circumstances. Consequently, a president can go through an entire term without knowing that some of his most trusted assistants have created resentments that have undermined his political position. He will, of course, read occasional articles in the newspapers describing the activities. These he is bound to regard as merely attacks by a jealous opposition, and the effect upon his thinking will be the reverse of what was intended.

A "strong" president, if strength is defined as determination to have one's own way, paradoxically is more liable to suffer from the operations of the White House staff system than one who is "weak." The strong man has a propensity to create an environment to his liking and to weed out ruthlessly those assistants who might persist in presenting him with irritating thoughts. It is no accident that White House staffs under the regime of a forceful president tend to become more and more colorless and more and more nondescript as time goes on. Palace-guard survivors learn early to camouflage themselves with a coating of battleship gray.

The "weak" president, on the other hand, is more susceptible to conflicting currents and less ready to eliminate strong-minded people from his immediate vicinity. The mere fact that he is somewhat "wishy-washy" at least assures that he will keep some avenues of approach open and that the courtier who has been cast out may find a way back in.

It is possible for a president to assemble a staff of mature men who are past the period of inordinate ambition that characterizes the courtier. But this is only a possibility—rarely, if ever, consummated. The White House is a court. Inevitably, in a battle between courtiers and advisers, the courtiers will win out. This represents the greatest of all barriers to presidential access to reality and raises a problem which will plague the White House so long as the president is a reigning monarch rather than an elected administrator.

★

VIII | THE PRESIDENCY AND THE PRESS

Of the few social institutions which tend to keep a president in touch with reality, the most effective—and the most resented by the chief beneficiary—is the press. It is the only force to enter the White House from the outside world with a direct impact upon the man in the Oval Room which cannot be softened by intermediary interpreters or deflected by sympathetic attendants.

This state of affairs does not arise out of any special integrity on the part of the press which, after all, is an institution manned by human beings subject to the same forces that govern human conduct generally. Neither does it spring from any unusual defenses or counterforces working against manipulation on the part of the president. It is simply a matter of the press function, which is to inform the public of the president's actions. No matter how sympathetically that function is performed, a foolish act will appear foolish, an unpopular act will arouse antagonism, and an act in conflict with previous actions will appear contradictory.

The significant impact of the press upon the president lies not in its critical reflections but in its capacity to tell him what he is doing as seen through other eyes. This is a service which, though little appreciated, is indispensable, as it will rarely, if ever, be performed by any other medium. Virtually all other communications that reach him will be shaped either directly or indirectly by people who wish either to conciliate or antagonize the chief executive. In either case, the contents of the message and the manner in which it is phrased will be governed as much by the sender's judgment of how best to produce a desired effect upon the recipient as by the substantive matters with which the sender deals.

Many newspaper stories and a much higher number of columns are written solely for their impact upon the president. Newspapermen are not exempt from the universal urge to shape history—or even to curry favor with an important element in their livelihood. But the newspaper itself is addressed to the public. If it is to survive, it must, on a daily basis, offer a reasonable presentation of events within certain bounds of accuracy and perspective. It cannot dedicate itself solely to the edification of one man, no matter how important that man may be. And while it can rearrange facts or interpret them in the best or worst possible light, its ability to *change* facts is severely limited as long as any degree of competition remains.

Presidents have considerable leverage with which to manipulate part of the press and all try to do so with varying degrees of success. The principal source of the leverage is the unusual position of the president as one of the very few figures in public life who has in his exclusive possession a type of news virtually indispensable to the social and economic security of any reporter assigned to cover the White House full time. This category of newsworthy material consists of the president himself—his

thoughts, his relationship with his friends and employees, his routine habits, his personal likes and dislikes,
his intimate moments with his family and his associates.
The fact that these things constitute "news" of a front-
page variety gives the president a trading power with
individual newsmen of such magnitude that it must be
seen at close quarters to be credited.

There is no other official of the government who can
make a top headline story merely by releasing a routine
list of his daily activities. There is no other official of the
government who can be certain of universal newspaper
play by merely releasing a picture of a quiet dinner with
boyhood friends. There is no other official who can attract
public attention merely by granting an interview consisting
of reflections, no matter how banal or mundane, on social
trends in fields where he has no expertise and in which his
concepts are totally irrelevant to his function as a public
servant.

It is not too hard for any other high official of the
government "to make news." But, with the exception of
notorious scandal, he can do so only through activities
which bear a direct relationship to his official function. A
secretary of state can command headlines by denouncing
the Soviet Union, but no one really cares about his views
on dogs. A secretary of labor can inspire widespread interest by commenting on a nationwide strike, but only in his
hometown is any newspaper likely to print a picture of him
playing with his grandson. An attorney general will receive respectful attention when he delivers an opinion on
crime in the streets, but no reporter will be credited with
an exclusive for revealing that he prefers Scotch to bour-
bon. As the interest of correspondents in government
officials extends primarily to their *public* acts, it is not

possible for those officials to monopolize the release of their activities. Consequently, the press can approach such officials on the basis of a total independence which cannot be sustained by those who cover the president. It is not at all unusual for newspapers to assign correspondents to cover cabinet agencies who are personally at odds with the heads of the agencies, but any responsible editor will have long second thoughts before assigning to the White House a man or a woman who has personally incurred presidential wrath or even the dislike of secretaries in the press office. Sometimes, long second thoughts will result in the assignment of the offending reporter anyway. But such occasions are rare.

The temptations inherent in this situation to "trade out"—to swap golden nuggets for "good" stories—are so overwhelming that few, if any, presidents of the modern era have been able to resist. It is taken for granted in the Washington press corps that there are certain "favorite" reporters who have "an in with the old man," as it is impossible for this state of affairs to be concealed for any great period of time. The press corps, in the early days of any administration, watches nervously for the first signs of a story that begins "the president is known to feel" or "the president has told close associates." There is a constant jockeying for a position which will permit the correspondent to deliver to his paper a set of exclusive photographs of the president and the First Lady walking in the White House garden (pictures taken by the official White House photographer). And the competition among the television networks for exclusive film reaches heights of savagery.

Any president would be well advised to resist the opportunities that are held forth so temptingly. Many presidents have been so advised. But it is not yet recorded that the advice has been accepted. The rewards of "trading out" are immediate and apparent. The penalties, which follow inexorably, are far down the road—so far down, in fact, that when they are exacted, it is difficult to trace back their origins. Every president who has played favorites has suffered in the long run. It is doubtful whether any of them will ever accept the truth of that statement. To understand it, it is necessary to back up for a moment and analyze the problem of presidential press relations.

A president's press problems are really quite simple. He does not have to make any extraordinary effort to attract attention. All channels of public communication are open to him any hour of the day or night. Every word that he utters will, sooner or later, find its way into print. If he does not like the paraphrases used by writing reporters, he can always take to the airwaves and the electronic media will deliver his exact language, with his own intonations, into every American home. He can keep newspapermen at his side twenty-four hours a day, if he so chooses, and he can depend upon their listening to his every argument. There is no other human being on the face of the globe who has any comparable facilities for projecting every thought, every nuance, that is in his mind.

Theodore Roosevelt considered the White House "a bully pulpit" and more than fifty years later an assistant wrote the phrase into a speech by Lyndon B. Johnson. It is likely that, left to his own devices, Johnson would have thought in terms of a magnificent stage—and the transition from pulpit to stage is one of the more significant trends in modern history.

A pulpit is a platform for persuasion and exhortation. A stage is a setting for a presentation which may or may not carry a message. It can be an instrument for education and leadership or an attention-getting device for entertainment.

As a stage, the White House has no equal in the electronic age. It is equipped with props that cannot be matched by Hollywood, Broadway, and Madison Avenue combined. It is staffed by technicians capable of solving the most difficult electronics problems in the wink of an eye. And above all, it has the faculty of commanding the instant and total attention of television networks that dominate the largest audience in all history.

In no other field is the power of a president so immediately apparent as in his relationship with the television networks. His slightest wish is treated as an imperial ukase, and no press secretary ever has to ask for time on the air. He need indicate only that the president will be available.

During the Johnson administration the networks went so far as to staff a highly expensive TV room in the White House with warm cameras manned throughout the working day. This gave the president the potential of appearing live on nationwide networks at a few minutes' notice, and the fact that he used the facility only rarely did not deter television executives from meeting high weekly bills for its operation.

Presented with instrumentalities like this, the average public-relations man planning an industrial or political campaign would, with justification, consider himself in seventh heaven. He would regard as absolutely ludicrous an assertion that he had a "press problem" (although he might be tempted to leave this impression with his client). And he would be absolutely correct. The reality is that a president has no press problems (except for a few minor administrative technicalities), but he does have political problems, all of which are reflected in their most acute form by the press.

Why, then, do presidents spend so much time discussing with their confidants—and sometimes with the public—their "press problems"? Why, then, have the relationships between presidents and the press over the years traveled such a rocky road? The answer involves some complicated and subtle points which no one comprehends completely but which are worthy of study not just in terms of the press but in terms of the presidency itself.

There is a deep-seated human tendency to confuse unhappy news with unhappy events and to assume that if the news can be altered, so can the events. This tendency is particularly accentuated among monarchs. As previously noted Peter the Great strangled the courier who brought him the tidings of the defeat at Narva. John F. Kennedy (or at least someone on his staff) cancelled the White House subscription to the *New York Herald Tribune*. The two acts were closely related and differed only in the degree of retaliation available to the two men.

At stake is a twentieth-century form of the word magic of primitive society. There is a widespread tendency to assume that the qualities that words represent can somehow be transferred to objects, regardless of their content. Thus, the advertising man holds, as an article of faith, that any stale idea will become "exciting" if the word "exciting" is drummed into the human consciousness a sufficient number of times by the electronic media. And similarly, it is assumed that a man somehow becomes "dedicated" and "forward looking" if he can just persuade people to associate the two adjectives with his name in print.

The techniques of word magic are unquestionably successful when they are applied to commodities which are necessities of life and which do not differ essentially from competing commodities, such as soap. Whether they apply in a more sophisticated environment is questionable. And whether they can override objective facts is something that has yet to be demonstrated. A president deals in objective facts. If the nation is at war, he must draft young men to risk their lives in battle. If the nation embarks on great projects, he must tax the people in order to finance the federal activities. When he makes the promises that all political leaders make in moments of euphoria, he arouses expectations that will not be quieted except through fulfillment.

It is only in George Orwell's world that war can be labeled peace; brutality labeled justice; economic misery labeled prosperity. Within the White House itself, of course, it is possible to apply much of the Orwellian formula with a high degree of success. No assistant or secretary has ever yet won an argument with a president—and very few have tried. It is entirely possible within the walls of 1600 Pennsylvania Avenue to create a universe that is utterly to the liking of the principal occupant. He will not go so far as to alter all facts. But he can be certain that the facts will be brought to him in the most sympathetic of forms and with the harshest blows softened. Within this atmosphere, the only grating note comes from the newspapers and the electronic media which are produced on the outside and which are not subject to rewriting. The *Congressional Record* and the White House record can be "corrected"—but not, at least at present, the record of the Fourth Estate.

Unfortunately for the mental peace of presidents,

events cannot be altered significantly by control over the printed word—at least not for any extended period of time. While the White House does have at its command instrumentalities for manipulating the press, they are effective only in regard to adjectives, not to the hard, substantive news that is the ultimate shaper of public opinion. Furthermore, the more successful the manipulation, the less useful becomes that part of the press which has been manipulated.

This situation arises out of the principal communications problem that faces every president—maintaining believability. The very factors that give the chief executive his tremendous advantage in the field of public relations also give him his greatest problem. It is simply that he is covered around the clock, with every word taken down and filed somewhere. Consequently, he is under the compulsion—if he is to be believed—of making his actions fit his words. Both his words and his actions make an extremely deep impression. He can lose the confidence of the people very quickly when the two do not coincide.

In this respect, a president is subjected to rules and to tests which do not apply to other types of political leaders. A senator can announce his ringing support of law and order in the streets of our cities without any fear of embarrassment over the future trend of crime statistics. But a president who makes the same statement must follow it up with action against muggers, thieves, and rapists and if the crime statistics do not go down, he is in trouble. A governor of a state can take a firm stand on cleaning up air pollution, and if the atmosphere remains foul he can explain to his constituents that the cause is the noisome discharge of sulphur-laden smoke from across the state line and there is nothing he can do about it. But a president who assumes a similar stance can never convince the American people that the problem is beyond his control.

In assessing a president, there is a deeply ingrained public assumption that his choices are determined by what he wants to do and what he does not want to do and he is, quite rightly, not accorded the benefit of the doubt when reality fails to measure up to his predictions. This is a very harsh test indeed, but there is a simple answer—presidents need not open their mouths until they have thought their way through the problem and devised workable solutions for which they need not apologize. It would be a great day for the country if this were to become the rule, but that is one day which will never arrive.

Idle words are a luxury in which no president can indulge. Of course, every presidential inauguration has been preceded by a campaign in which the promises are, at the very least, extravagant. Fortunately, the beginning of a term is marked by a public willingness to give the new president every opportunity, and if he uses this "honeymoon period" to establish his credibility, he can look forward to a relatively secure eight-year tenure in office.

The classic story of the gap between promise and performance goes back to the political grand master Franklin D. Roosevelt. In the 1932 campaign he promised the American people that he would cut governmental spending and balance the budget—a foolish promise which was forgotten almost immediately after the New Dealers entered Washington, frantic in their desire to deliver some relief to the depression-stricken populace. A torrent of spending measures spewed out of the Capitol in the famous "100 Days" of FDR. Republicans, as soon as they recovered from their shock over the magnitude of their defeat, launched a campaign to remind Mr. Roosevelt publicly of his promises to cut spending. The principal promise had been made in a speech in Pittsburgh, and after a few days of particularly vehement GOP attack, Mr. Roosevelt called in his adviser Judge Samuel Rosenman and asked him to study the speech and produce an explanation. Mr. Rosenman returned in a matter of hours and said: "Mr. President, there is only one way to explain this speech. Deny that you ever made it!"

Fortunately, Mr. Roosevelt was still in the "honeymoon" period and the problems confronting the American people were so great that no one really cared about budget cutting. He was never again, however, granted such leeway and he quickly learned to match words with action and to forgo statements, or at least make them so fuzzy that they were incomprehensible, when he clearly lacked the resources to back his promises. As has been stated many times in this book, Mr. Roosevelt was a remarkable man who learned even from his own mistakes. This is one trait that few of his predecessors or his successors emulated.

Furthermore, the influence of a president is so great that people very soon identify those who are known as his "spokesmen." He eventually finds thoughts and programs attributed to him solely because they appeared in the columns of "pet" newspapermen. When those newspapermen move to his defense in print, their explanations of his actions are suspect and discounted in the opinion of presidential observers.

It is actually dangerous for a newspaperman to have a close personal friendship with a political leader. Such unfortunates find themselves identified as "sycophants" regardless of how scrupulous they are in handling their contacts. One of the outstanding examples is the columnist William S. White, a man of massive integrity, whose fortunes declined under the Lyndon Johnson administration simply because of a friendship with the president which dated back more than thirty-five years. White, whose politics were far more conservative than those of the president, found that he could not write as forcefully as he wished on many subjects without embarrassing the White House because his words were interpreted as emanating from the Oval Room. His circulation actually picked up when Johnson left the White House because people started to read him for what *he* was saying rather than for what they thought the *president* was saying, and he had a natural audience for his point of view.

Even more important is the fact that since manipulation of the press involves favoritism to some newsmen it inevitably creates antagonism among others. There is an old political rule which is generally stated: "Every time a man does a favor he makes nineteen enemies and one ingrate." Obviously, favors cannot be done for every member of the press or they would become meaningless. For every newspaperman who is placed in an advantageous position, several others must be placed in a disadvantageous position. Every president who plays the game inevitably winds up with more enemies than friends.

Basically, however, the long-standing antagonism between presidents and the press has deeper roots than the childish games that the White House usually plays with the Washington press corps. It is more validly traced to the fundamental dichotomy of interest that exists between newspapermen and politicians. No amount of manipulation can ever produce newspapers that are satisfactory to political leaders, or politicians who are satisfactory to newspapermen (unless George Orwell's nightmare, in which politicians had the capacity not only to produce newspapers but to rewrite the newspapers of the past, comes to fruition). A few words are necessary on this point.

Politicians, as a class, are dedicated to changing the world. With very few exceptions, they have in their minds some bright and shining ideal which is so obviously superior to what exists that it seems to be reality, with the actual world around them merely some kind of an aberration. Newspapermen, on the other hand, are held, to some degree, to the facts. They can play with adjectives; they can arrange the facts in any order that suits their convenience; they can give their prejudices full sway. But it is still their principal mission to present the world as it is. The two points of view are fundamentally incompatible.

Since the politician is oriented toward changing the world, he is constantly in a search for help. He divides the people with whom he must deal into friend or foe—those who have a "constructive" attitude and those who are purely "aginners." To have any force and effect as a political leader, he must be a partisan. And no partisan ever seized and maintained a position of power on the basis of self-examination and inner doubts. An Adlai Stevenson could arouse the respect and admiration of millions of people, but, like Hamlet who never became king, he never became president and it is doubtful that there is any conceivable set of circumstances under which he would ever have achieved the prize.

It is an article of faith with most politicians that any newspaper item even remotely touching upon the government was written through partisan inspiration, not just because it happened. The concept that there are professional standards which determine news leads and news placement is alien to their view of society.

In justice, it must be recognized that a large proportion of political stories originate with a choice morsel leaked to the press for a partisan purpose. The Washington reporter who does not play Democrats off against Republicans and vice versa is simply ignoring a fundamental tool of his trade and is not destined for success. An occasional plug in return for a hot item is considered within the bounds of ethical conduct.

But the politician's view of the press is not limited to recognition of this obvious aspect of the game. He refuses to concede that there are events which will find their way into newspapers without any partisan help whatsoever. Moreover, he is incapable of crediting newsmen with the ability to make simple deductions unassisted by people with an ax to grind.

An illustrative incident which stays vividly in my mind took place in the late 1940s when I was a reporter for the United Press. The Democrats had just recaptured Congress after two years of Republican domination and the interregnum had produced some interesting shifts in the Democratic hierarchy. Among other things, the inexorable workings of the seniority system had placed Representative William L. Dawson of Illinois in the top spot on the House Executive Expenditures Committee. Since Mr. Dawson was the first Negro to be in this position since Reconstruction, this was news by any standard, particularly as the committee had broad investigative powers. Furthermore, there were a number of Southern members in the group.

A poll of the committee was practically a reflex action. My first call was to a Southern congressman. My question was simply whether there would be any trouble. The response was a snarl: "When did [some name unknown to me] reach you?" I was completely taken aback—even more so when I discovered that the congressman, with whom I had reasonably cordial relations, was referring to a small-town lawyer who was building an opposition political machine in his district. He accepted my statement that I had never heard of his foe but remained unshaken in his conviction that someone had "told" me there would be trouble or I would not have phoned him. His conviction was reinforced later in the day when he was called with the identical query by members of other wire services and newspapers. This, to him, was proof of conspiracy, not simply evidence that professional newsmen were reacting to a professional standard of judgment. (It should be added that the committee poll disclosed no opposition to Mr. Dawson and the stories that were written merely stated that he would become chairman.)

There are very few politicians who do not cherish privately the notion that there should be some regulation of the news. To most of them, "freedom of the press" is a gigantic put-on, a clever ploy which has enabled publishers as an economic group in our society to conduct themselves with a degree of arrogance and disregard of the public interest that is denied to other groups. The "ploy" has succeeded to an extent where it cannot be challenged publicly and therefore must be accorded formal deference. But the deference is purely formal and rarely expressed with heartfelt enthusiasm.

If censorship ever comes to the United States, it will explode out of the frustrations of a political leader convinced that the public good is being thwarted by self-serving reporters distorting the news. It will be the culmination of the natural political instinct to extend to the press the same standards he applies to the rest of society—does this help or hurt a worthy cause? The crusader is much more likely to sound the death knell of free expression than the cynic.

The great game of politics is a highly personal pursuit in which official activity and social amenities are inextricably intermingled. A politician really does not expect a fellow human being to sell his soul for a handshake or a free barbecue. But he is always hurt and bewildered when the recipient of the shake or the beef responds in a mood that he interprets as antagonistic. This attitude is extended not only to other politicians but to businessmen, professionals, clergymen, and the press. It is impossible for newspapermen—even those who are psychologically disposed to walk in the footsteps of the world's oldest profession—to respond on every occasion with what the political leader regards as an appropriately grateful reciprocity. Therefore, in the politician's mind newspapermen are invariably guilty of "ingratitude." Furthermore, politicians look to members of the press to be "constructive," to help them put across worthwhile programs for the betterment of humanity. It should be added, in all justice, that this is strikingly similar to the attitude of civic leaders, who always begin any crusade for municipal betterment by calling upon the editor of the local newspaper and asking him to "get behind" it.

The concept of a "constructive reporter" is a contradiction in terms. A newspaperman who selects his stories on the basis of "the national interest" is actually doing the national interest a disservice. He has no business making such decisions. The closest he can come to it and still remain true to his trade is to report what others conceive to be "in the national interest." This is a point which no successful politician can grasp.

Frequently, newspapers themselves fail to grasp the

point. The classic case is the downplaying by the *New York Times* of the projected invasion of the Bay of Pigs in Cuba. Here was an instance where those who decided to temper the news were thoroughly convinced that they were acting "in the national interest" because if they featured the story, the invasion would have been called off. They did not feature the story, the invasion did take place, the result was a debacle because of inadequate planning, and American prestige dipped to a new low.

This, of course, will not serve in the slightest to convince political leaders of the future that newspapers should place reporting of the news ahead of what they consider to be "the national interest." It is impossible for them to think otherwise. The political leader who rises to the top moves through a world which is sharply delineated between those who are helping him; those who are opposing him; and those who are uncommitted but can be swung in any direction. His success has been based upon the manipulation of these three groups to achieve what he regards as fulfillment of the national interest—and such manipulation is, in most instances, entirely legitimate. The whole political process would break down and democratic government would be impossible without the existence of men skilled in this art. To persuade them that the press should be an exception would be pushing their credulity beyond human limits.

Furthermore, the politician is a human being subject to the normal tendency to overgeneralize from his own experiences. He knows that some members of the press can be manipulated. Therefore, he assumes that those who resist his blandishments have simply been reached first by a competitor. He is consciously encouraged in this belief by the newspapermen who "play ball" with him.

The importance of a "source" can be measured not only by its news value but by the degree of its exclusivity. To maintain his position in his industry, a reporter must display professional competence in judging and presenting the news. But to advance, he must also demonstrate a capacity to obtain information unavailable to others—or at least available only on a restricted or delayed basis. There are both positive and negative paths that can be followed in achieving this capacity, and the artful journalist is capable of following both courses.

The positive path is to persuade important newsmakers that they can have confidence in the manner in which the reporter will handle a story. The newsman presents himself as one who will not divulge off-the-record material; who will not embarrass his informant by identifying his source; who will not twist the facts to present an event in an unfavorable light. This approach is vital to a successful reporting career and is not to be disdained.

The negative path is consciously to feed the paranoia that characterizes virtually every politician to some degree. A few words of sympathy over the unfair treatment by the "Eastern press" (or the liberal press or the conservative press) is an effective method of slamming doors against competitors. An important leader who can be persuaded that his journalistic "friend" is the lone holdout against a "press conspiracy" can serve as a meal ticket for many years.

Since the press as a whole cannot be "won over" by tactics which political leaders regard as legitimate, it is inevitable that newspapermen eventually become the "enemy." In addition, they also become the personification of all the frustrating forces that make the life of a president so difficult. Therefore, over a period of time, it is certain that the political leader will vent his spleen against the press, never realizing that what he is really doing is venting his spleen against the whole intractable environment that surrounds him. It is a very easy matter to find legitimate grounds for criticizing the press. It is a less easy matter to realize that all these grounds apply to the world generally.

Every president has his collection of inaccuracies in press coverage and is willing to regale his listeners by recounting them for hours. Seen in perspective, these inaccuracies are usually trivial and reflect merely the fact that reporters are human beings who are bound to make errors under the constant pressure of reporting world-shaking events almost as soon as they happen. An objective evaluation would be that the degree of accuracy with which the news is reported is astounding when it is contrasted with the conditions under which it is gathered. But a politician smarting under the lash of public criticism is not very likely to be objective.

Every president has his horror stories of press arrogance. But press arrogance is merely a reflection of public arrogance. Almost every American feels qualified to give the president advice on the most complicated and subtle questions of economics, law, and international relations. It would be surprising if newspapermen were exempt from this universal temptation.

Every president can recite valid examples of press bias and is entitled legitimately to some sympathy for the manner in which he is treated by opposition newspapers. But the assumption that bias is a journalistic characteristic rather than a condition of humanity is a distorted view of the universe. When a man enters politics, he undertakes to deal with *all* human characteristics and it is not an acceptable alibi to cite some of them as overwhelming. If press bias were an absolute bar to political success, this nation would never have had an Abraham Lincoln, and Franklin D. Roosevelt and Harry S Truman would have been denied second terms.

In reality, the problem of a president in dealing with the press is precisely the same as his problem in dealing with the public at large. But no president can find it within his ego to concede that he has failed in any degree with the public. It is far more satisfying to blame his failures on the press because his problems then can be attributed to a conspiracy. He can blame the "Eastern press," the "Republican press," or the "liberal press." He then does not stand indicted within his own consciousness (the most terrible court of all) as having failed. He was merely the victim of vindictiveness on the part of a selfish group and his failure can be attributed to the meanness of others rather than to his own inadequacies.

In the mythical world of philosopher-kings, the press policies of the White House would be very simple indeed. They would consist solely and simply of according all media equal access to whatever information was available. The philosopher-king would realize that the press is merely a part of the public, even though it is charged with some special functions in the nation's economy. Unfortunately, we do not live in the world of philosopher-kings and it is unlikely that we ever will.

★

IX | THE FIFTH WHEEL

The American political party, in the traditional view held by most of our citizens, would seem to be an ideal instrumentality for keeping a president in touch with reality. It is seen as earthy, grass roots, intensely pragmatic— a world inhabited by cigar-chewing characters who seek only to keep the people happy so they can stay in power and who care nothing about ideological niceties. It is unfortunate that in national terms the picture does not accord with observable fact, whatever may be the structures at local levels.

From a national standpoint, a party in power belongs to the president. It is his to do with as he sees fit—to use it, abuse it, or ignore it altogether. He appoints the national chairman, dominates the national committee, and determines the extent and character of its activities. Members of the national staff come to see him, hat in hand, in no mood to raise perplexing and troublesome questions. And he can, if he so desires, appoint assistants who will count every postage stamp used by that staff.

This situation arises primarily out of the basic nature of the American political party. It is not an ideological in-

strument nor does it have "members," in the European
sense of the word. It is purely a technical convenience
which is used by candidates to supply funds and workers
for election campaigns. There is no genuine inner party life
between conventions at the national level except for the
jockeyings of a few partisan bureaucrats to attain some
degree of proximity to the president. When a party is out
of power, the jockeying becomes more interesting. It
still goes on through frantic efforts to become close to the
"leader." Since no one can identify this person with certainty, it is something like playing blindfold chess with no
one calling off the opponent's moves or announcing
"check" and "checkmate."

Traditionally, the American political party has been
held in very low esteem, except by newly arrived immigrant groups who have found in their ward leaders the
only sympathetic help available to guide them in bewildering circumstances. A few of the higher offices, such as
national committeeman, are sought by "respectable" citizens—chiefly because they involve at least one presidential
reception a year. But generally, "politics" has been regarded as something in which a "gentleman" will not engage. It has been a domain reserved for the very crass
or the very young whose elders assume that they will get
over their fling of youthful idealism and engage in more
acceptable pursuits.

The result has been an increasing tendency to stray
outside the party machinery for political assistance even
in campaign years. Most presidents look to "citizens' committees" and "scientists' committees" plus a host of others
with a "nonpartisan" tinge, as their most effective political
aids. Partially, of course, this trend is due to restrictive

campaign laws, which make a proliferation of committees essential for fund-raising purposes. But even more important, it reflects a feeling that many citizens are repelled by a political party. They want their presidents to be untouched by the muck of partisanship.

Presidents are probably correct in their judgment on the efficacy of nonpartisan election machinery. It is an excellent source of otherwise unobtainable votes, and men campaigning for office tend to hold such sources in very high regard. Unfortunately, it also means that a successful candidate is unlikely to regard the party machinery as something to which he should pay much attention after he is in office. It did not appear to him crucial during the campaign (presidents are usually convinced that they won their elections single-handed anyway) and it appears irrelevant to the high problems of statecraft that enter the Executive Mansion so intoxicatingly. Therefore, another source of access to hard reality is closed off. It is not even replaced by the solemn nonpartisan committees composed of distinguished citizens which fold up as soon as they have paid off their debts.

This status is dimly sensed by the groups of young people who are urging so vehemently what they call "the politics of participation." They feel that there should be some kind of yeasty ferment in daily political life, something other than a chance to blow horns, pop balloons, and strain larynxes every four years. They are right—dead right— but they are not going to get it through "party reform." What is needed is basic change in the presidency itself, and this is not going to come through the action of the national committees. The inner political life is not going to be yeasty so long as the men in power do not have to listen. There will be no participatory politics when a president can so easily separate himself from the partisan process.

A closely related problem has been raised by the academicians. There have been few subjects more hotly discussed among the academic fraternity of political scientists in the past thirty years than that of "party responsibility." But, with a few notable exceptions, the bulk of the discussion has ignored totally the determining factor in whether it is possible to have "responsible" political parties at all—the office of the presidency.

The framework of government is basically a group of appropriate channels through which power relationships can be exercised. The art of politics is the effort to seize and occupy key positions in that framework. Therefore, it would seem to be a truism that the limits of legal political activity within a society would be established by the framework of government. But this truism is apparently too elementary to have made an impact on the political thinking of many academicians. They have assumed that the character of political parties can be determined by conscious acts of will, that a group of people can form a party of predetermined character and use it as a vehicle for securing power. This is a grossly oversimplified view. But it is an oversimplification which has dominated political discussion and which has rarely been examined.

It is necessary to define the term "responsible" political party for the discussion to have any meaning whatsoever. As the term is used among students of government, it means an ideological party—one whose platform can be read in the secure knowledge that if the party achieves power it will act, or try to act, according to the planks that had been set forth.

The United States has had many such parties in the course of its political history. There have been the Populist party, the Greenback party, the Socialist party, the Socialist Labor party, the Communist party, the Prohibition party, and a number of others too numerous to have achieved more than a footnote in erudite studies of the political process. Some of those parties have secured widespread popular support for a brief period. But invariably, all have disappeared, either by absorption into one of the major parties or by simply lapsing into limbo. The more successful, such as the Farmer-Labor party in Minnesota or the Progressive party in Wisconsin, have succeeded in making a formal alliance with either the Democrats or the Republicans. Others, such as the Socialist party, converted themselves into discussion groups. One, the Liberal party of New York, has managed to survive for a lengthy period but only as a broker of convenience offering voters a simplified method of splitting their tickets.

By many of the academic political scientists, the inability of these parties to survive has been treated as a form of mental aberration on the part of the electorate. They have assumed that there was a demand for such parties and that the only issue was to find the correct set of ideological proposals with sufficient appeal to put one of those parties into power. What they have ignored is a fundamental reality of the American political structure that permits the continued existence of two parties—and two parties only.

This reality is the inability of the executive branch to form a coalition. The Constitution of the United States lodges *all* executive authority in the hands of one man and there is no form of human ingenuity which can transform one man into a coalition.

This factor is basic and determining. Democratic government is inconceivable except through a coalition. There are too many differing approaches to every issue to permit any one point of view to hold more than a fleeting majority. Stable government can be achieved only through the processes of accommodation. And when a form of government specifically prohibits such an accommodation from being made, the inevitable necessity of coalition requires that the accommodation be at another level. It is for this reason that America's major political parties are essentially coalitions—and can only be coalitions.

The enduring political parties of the United States are almost entirely the result of historical events followed by evolutionary development. At times they have taken on ideological aspects. The Republican party was almost certainly formed as a result of the Free Soil movement of the 1850s, but it cannot be stated categorically that the GOP came into being solely as an antislavery party. Whatever its origins may have been, it certainly did not continue in that vein. As for the Democratic party, determining its origins is almost entirely a question of historical interpretation. Democratic orators refer to themselves in stentorian tones as the offspring of Jefferson and Jackson. But it takes a real act of uncritical faith to connect the labor-farmer-liberal-immigrant coalition formed by Franklin D. Roosevelt with the frontier agrarian radicalism of Jefferson and Jackson. The real basis for the continued existence of both parties lies even today in sectional, social, and economic loyalties, although sectional and social ties are breaking down rapidly under the impact of industrial interdependency.

For many years, professional politicians found themselves embarrassed on any college campus by a simple request for a definition of the differences between the two parties. The question should not truly have been embarrassing because it was based upon a false premise—that America's political parties resembled the ideological groupings of Europe. The professional politicians made the mistake of accepting the premise and on that basis they were lost. They could resort only to generalities about the "party of progress" or the "party of stability"—generalities not very impressive to youthful minds which have not yet fallen into the mental ruts that sometimes go with maturity. An honest answer to the question would have been that the Democratic party has continuing trouble with left-wing crackpots and the Republican party has continuing trouble with right-wing crackpots. But the honest answer is not the respectable answer. Therefore the professionals left the question shrouded in mystery.

In so doing, they performed a disservice to the American political system by making it look ridiculous. It is not ridiculous, although I feel intensely that some very fundamental changes are necessary. It is a totally logical system which reacts to the necessities of the power relationships in our society. And one of these reactions is the coalition political party.

The party platform is an outstanding example of a rational activity by a coalition party which has been condemned as futile by academicians because of failure to understand fundamental premises. It is usually damned as an expression of pious generalities that has no purpose other than to mislead the electorate with sugar-coated promises—and that generally fails to achieve that purpose. Political commentators emphasize continuously throughout a campaign that the presidential candidates are paying little or no attention to the platform and will pay even less attention to it in the event that they are elected. This latter criticism is accurate but totally irrelevant. It is irrelevant because it assumes that the purpose of a party platform is to tell the voters what the party will do once it is in power. Nothing could be farther from the reality. The true purpose of a party platform is to determine the outer limits under which the coalition can be held together, and the intense fighting which goes on at every party convention is a reflection of this purpose.

The party platform has served its purpose the moment it is adopted. It has provided the arena within which contending ideological factions have decided whether they will "stay in" or "walk out." This may seem a roundabout way of making that determination but it would really be difficult to devise a better mechanism. The ruling hierarchy of a political party must determine somehow the price of maintaining unity and must pass judgment upon whether that price is worth paying. There is no reliable guide other than to raise issues of gut emotion and then watch the partisans as they negotiate acceptable language. Sometimes, as in the Democratic convention of 1948, the party decides that the price is too high and permits a walkout by some of the delegates. In this instance, it proved to be a wise decision and the party went ahead to win the election. In 1912, however, the Republican party made a decision that the price of unity was too high and the resulting party split enabled the Democrats to elect their second president since the Civil War. Regardless of the wisdom of either decision, however, it is obvious that the decision had to be made.

The necessity for coalition political parties is so obvious to the average professional politician that he is unable, as a general rule, even to engage in a rational dialogue on the subject with the academic fraternity. Any such discussion—and a number have been held over the years—invariably erupts in a free-for-all. The professional politician understands instinctively the premises of the coalition party but is incapable of articulating them. The academic political scientist understands the need for ideological parties, but except in rare instances appears incapable of comprehending the necessary conditions for forming them. Someday, this gulf of understanding must be crossed so that the two groups can work together to devise a system that gives greater weight to ideology.

It is essential, in this connection, to distinguish between coalition government and bipartisanship. The concept of bipartisanship occupies a hallowed position in American political folklore, but its only practical effect has been to increase the strength of some presidents under some circumstances. The most revered part of the folklore has been that of the bipartisan foreign policy. It is assumed that somehow politics should end "at the water's edge" and that the foreign policy of the United States should reflect the will of *all* the people. This fantastic bit of nonsense (fantastic because it never has and never will be true) has been accepted only because the word "partisan" is pejorative in our vocabulary, and people shrink from applying it to crucial decisions. The Constitution of the United States gives the president exclusive control over foreign policy, subject only to certain checks. A president is, almost by definition, a political man. There is no rational basis for assuming that he is going to be "bipartisan" about fiscal policy, labor policy, farm policy, or any other issue upon which differing views are possible. He may, of course, turn to members of the other party for advice on foreign affairs, but he is just as likely to turn to those members for advice on the other issues. Actually, there is no mechanism whatsoever in the American system whereby a policy of any kind can be made "bipartisan" because our political parties cannot negotiate meaningful agreements on matters of substance. No one can state with certainty who officially represents a political party when it does not control the presidency. It is possible to deal with the congressional leaders of a minority party or with some of its governors. But none of them can "speak" for their party in any authoritative sense. The cold fact is that when a Democratic president consults Republicans, he is consulting them in their status as interested American citizens or, at most, in their capacity as representatives of small groups of Republicans, and not as ideological representatives of the GOP.

So-called bipartisan government, as actually practiced in the United States, rests upon a grant of status to members of another party by a political leader who is in power. Sometimes it is wise for him to grant such status; sometimes it is unwise. But under either set of circumstances it is something he can do or undo by a conscious act of will. A true coalition represents status which men can exact as a price for cooperation because of the political power at their command. If an Italian cabinet includes members of a minority party, it is because the members of the majority party do not have enough political power to form a government without the help of the minority. There just isn't anything else that can be done.

Under the American constitutional system, there are no forces which can *compel* a president of the United States to allocate positions to members of the minority party in order to hang on to the presidency. The president himself represents the monopoly of ultimate, executive power. He serves by tenure and nothing short of the complicated procedures of impeachment or the Twenty-fifth

Amendment can remove him from office. He keeps the reins of presidential power in his hands even if his following in the country has shrunk to 10 percent or to zero. And even if, as an act of political wisdom, he places minority members in his cabinet they enter as *his* agents—not the agents of their party. Their partisan affiliations have no more relevancy to their administration of office than their church affiliations or their social ties.

A major example of this kind of bipartisanship came during World War II, when Franklin D. Roosevelt placed Republicans in his cabinet—Henry L. Stimson and Frank Knox, Secretaries of War and Navy, respectively. It was a very shrewd move by any standard. It nailed down the concept that the conduct of the war was an enterprise in which the president deserved the support of all of the people regardless of their attitude toward his politics. It disarmed opposition and gave Roosevelt elbow room which he would not otherwise have had. It was also an entirely safe move. Neither Stimson nor Knox represented the Republican party in the Roosevelt cabinet any more than they represented the legal profession or newspaper publishing. They became solely agents of the president, administering key agencies under his personal direction and control. At the time of the appointments, many Republicans muttered (quite rightly) over what they regarded as a "trick" to disarm them as an opposition party. Mr. Stimson and Mr. Knox underwent considerable criticism from their fellow members of the GOP, but the criticism was muted. It was not politic to fault the president on what appeared to be a tremendous gesture of farsighted goodwill and "bipartisanship."

Since that time, it has become commonplace for presidents to place members of the other party in their cabinets. The gesture has been taken for granted, so much so that it scarcely causes the lift of an eyebrow or a slight ripple in the political community. There was even some perfunctory criticism of Mr. Nixon for not naming a Democrat to his first cabinet. The American people have adjusted to the idea, realizing that it does not represent a coalition in any true sense of the word and is known as "bipartisanship" only through a very loose use of the term.

The lack of clear-cut ideological parties is also stressed by the president's relationship to the Congress. The president does not "control" Congress at any time, not even at periods of great popularity when it is politic for most legislators to go along with him. His true relationship to Congress is basically that of a highly important factor which the legislators must take into account. When the president's popularity is immense, he represents the major factor and can get pretty much what he wants regardless of the political composition of either branch. As soon as his poll ratings start to slip, Congress reasserts its independence. It is quite apparent that the question of whether the president has a majority of his own party in the Congress is academic. What matters is whether his following on both sides of the legislative aisle constitutes a majority.

Harry S Truman served as president for two full years with a Congress dominated by the opposite party. He managed to convince the public at the end of those two years that the Congress had been so obstructive that he was entitled to a Democratic Congress as well as re-election. But an objective appraisal of the Eightieth (Republican) Congress will inevitably lead to the conclusion that it was much more productive than Harry Truman would ever admit.

The Eightieth Congress forced into law the Taft-

Hartley Act and the two-term presidential limitation over Mr. Truman's objections. On the other hand it gave him the British aid bill, the Truman Doctrine (for Greece and Turkey), and the Marshall Plan. The latter, by any criteria, represented superior acts of statesmanship and a high degree of cooperation. The two Democratic Congresses which followed were certainly far less cooperative and far less productive.

Dwight D. Eisenhower, as a Republican, served the last three-quarters of his presidency with Democratic Congresses and in the first quarter his Republican majority was of a hairline quality. Nevertheless, no one could maintain seriously that he was blocked or frustrated in any important particular by the Democrats. Lyndon B. Johnson, the Democratic leader of the Senate during the Eisenhower administration, actually built his reputation as a national statesman by continuously putting congressional Republicans in an obstructive light and Eisenhower in a position where he was rescued time and time again by Democrats from the machinations of his own party. It was a tactic which worked because it was valid. The Democrats were much more sympathetic to Eisenhower than were the members of his own party.

The fact that the coalition system works among American political parties, however, is not sufficient reason to conclude that the coalition parties are ideal by any stretch of the imagination. They have been under heavy criticism from political scientists for many years and the criticisms are justified.

They do not give Americans a sufficiently clear choice.

They do not provide an outlet for large segments of the population who feel excluded from the major parties.

They reduce political discussion to a low level of pious generalities which ill prepare the American people for the problems that lie ahead.

In the 1968 campaign, for example, the only candidate who really discussed the issues that were moving the American people was the third-party representative, George Wallace. The fact that his discussion was the "wrong" discussion, that he was a dangerous demagogue arousing ugly emotions, should not be allowed to obscure the fact that he had a virtual monopoly in talking about the things that counted. Both Mr. Nixon and Mr. Humphrey debated questions on the basis of generalities and emotional appeals to past loyalties. They were quite wise to do so. They knew that coalition parties offered no adequate platform for pointed discussions. Mr. Wallace, on the other hand, labored under no such handicap. His own political platform had been created especially for him and he did not have to worry about any sizable group of people walking out. By the same token, however, he had no possibility of winning the election because his fundamental approach was too divisive.

In the United States, true ideological discussion is something that never takes place at the political party level. Americans thresh out their ideological differences in other forums—in labor unions, in women's clubs, in newspaper columns (including letters to the editor), in farm cooperatives, and in other organizations which are not constrained by the necessity of holding together coalescing forces. It is assumed at a national convention that ideological problems have been aired before the delegates got anywhere near the place and that no minds are going to be changed by intellectual persuasion. The convention itself becomes an arena in which the ideological blocs can test their strength and determine what accommodations they must make in order to secure their maximum influence within the party.

This is the factor that has led to the elaborate "ticket balancing" which always characterizes the party team. A "liberal" Democrat is quite likely to name a more conservative vice-presidential candidate; a Western Republican is more likely to look east for his running mate. This, of course, has real value in terms of stressing national unity and helping the winning candidate to start off his presidential term with some hope of achieving a consensus. But it also leads all too frequently to the selection of admittedly inferior men over admittedly superior men. The superior men are bypassed simply because they do not help to hold the party coalition together.

Perhaps the problems of ideological parties in the American system can best be seen by a look at Congress. On a number of occasions, minor parties have succeeded in electing representatives and senators. When I first began covering the nation's legislature as a newspaperman, the Senate included two members of the Farmer-Labor party, one member of the Progressive party, and one independent. The House contained a number of Farmer-Laborites and Progressives and one member of the American Labor party. All of them were, strictly speaking, a bloody nuisance to the officials of Congress charged with the housekeeping functions of that body. It was not possible to build separate cloakrooms for the minor-party members. Patronage problems were insuperable—how do you give a member of the American Labor party 1/435th of a pageboy?— and the Republican and Democratic leadership opened every session with an endless wrangle about how the minor-party members were to receive their committee assignments. These, of course, were all housekeeping problems which only represented headaches. But they were also revealing of the fact that the American system is not capable of coping easily with more than two political parties—one in power and one in opposition.

None of this is to be construed as persuasive argument against ideological political groupings. In fact, it is becoming increasingly apparent that there are pressures in our society for such groupings. The "McCarthyite" revolt in the Democratic party of 1968 represented a strong surge of people who were not ideologically satisfied with what remained of the coalition of Franklin D. Roosevelt. The Republican presidential nomination of Barry Goldwater in 1964 was clearly a successful effort of ideologically motivated people to find a political voice. Both efforts ended in electoral failure and, in fact, were doomed to failure even before they had started. The ultimate objective of these political drives was the capture of executive power, which, under the American system, is held by one man. There was no constitutional way in which the ideologues of either the McCarthy or the Goldwater persuasion could obtain a measure of relief from their frustrations by securing some part of the executive power. The battle for the presidency is an "all or nothing" proposition, and the losers are left out in the cold for another four years. Unless executive power can somehow be dispersed through cabinet officials, under a system whereby they hold their positions because they have gained them through political struggle, ideological groupings will remain deprived of an adequate outlet.

The arguments for responsible party government are compelling. But their logic is totally irrelevant so long as the end result of political activity is elevation to the presidency and so long as the president is a man with a complete monopoly of ultimate answers and with no direct responsibility to another elected body. Those who desire ideological politics must await the day when mechanisms are available which permit coalition at the government level, and thereby relieve our political parties of the necessity of filling this role.

★

X | TO TINKER WITH THE MACHINERY

It is very obvious at the time of this writing that the American people sense the institution of the presidency to be in trouble. An office that was taken for granted a few short years ago has now become the object of critical study by political scientists, commentators, editorial writers, and former presidents and their assistants. Some scholars—such as Richard Neustadt and Clinton Rossiter—have devoted entire careers to analyses of the position. The presidency has been placed under more microscopes than any other similar office in history.

From the standpoint of the general public, of course, the feeling of uneasiness can be traced directly to the identification of the presidency with the nation. The troubles of our country are painfully apparent. The war in Vietnam still chews up our youth. Our college students are on rampages without precedent in our history. Inflation is bringing millions of Americans close to the edge of economic hardship. Negro militants are challenging not only their past inferiority in a segregated society but the validity of the liberal dream of a fully integrated society.

Should President Nixon succeed in pulling out of

Vietnam and re-establishing some degree of internal stability, much of the uneasiness of the general public would be allayed. But the causes which gave rise to the restlessness would remain. They would merely be less apparent with some of the stresses and strains removed.

Very little of the public discussion has focused on what I believe to be the major problem of the presidency, the increasing tendency of the office to isolate its occupant from reality. Instead, the assumption has been that the problems of our government could be solved by taking the president even further out of the political arena, removing some of the ability of the Congress to frustrate his will, and giving him more technical help. On this basis, the proposals which have received the most widespread attention in recent years would:

Restrict the president to one six-year term.

Extend the term of members of the House of Representatives to four years so they would always be running with a presidential candidate at the top of the ticket.

Appoint "assistant presidents" to take some of the burdens out of the hands of the chief executive.

The proposal for "assistant presidents" can be dismissed out of hand. It is inconceivable that any president would ever permit another to have a piece of his power, even if practical machinery could be devised to make it possible. But the first two proposals deserve some extended consideration. Both were given a heavy impetus by the last administration and both are remedies in the classic style of the "hair of the dog."

These proposals are designed to lessen the political pressures that bear upon the presidency. The first assumes that if a president could not run for a second term, he would concentrate all his efforts on running the country. The second assumes that he would not have to face balky Congresses if the members had to run on the same ticket with him. In either case, he would not have to worry about hostile people threatening him with reprisals at the polls.

There is a naïveté about these proposals which would be charming in its innocence if so much were not at stake. They assume that wise and effective government flows from careful study by responsible men who have access to "all" the facts and who need only the authority and the machinery to carry out intelligently designed programs. In this concept, the bar to heaven on earth lies in the capacity of lesser informed, and sometimes selfish, mortals to frustrate the nation's administrators by political manipulation.

It is not surprising that these proposals should come from the "activists." Political advocates always work (and must always work) on the assumption that truth is an absolute rather than the product of shoving and hauling by competing intellectual interests. They live in a world of "right" and "wrong," categories which are entirely adequate for the conduct of political affairs from any platform except a throne or the White House. And for partisans, there can be no explanation for being "wrong" except lack of knowledge or venality.

The proposal for a six-year term is particularly interesting because it is based on the belief that a president's authority is somehow separable from his political leadership. It regards the nation as a corporate enterprise which can be managed without regard to the feelings of the employees or the stockholders (an obsolete view of corporate structure) and it assumes that a president does what he wants to do merely by issuing orders.

The reality is quite different. A president whose political leadership is unchallenged can do just about anything that he wishes. A president whose political leadership has suffered from erosion is virtually helpless. And one of the factors of political leadership is the assumption by those with whom he deals that he will be in office for a long time to come. In this respect, the six-year proposal would not even accomplish the ends sought by its proponents.

A six-year president would be a "lame duck" from the moment he took the oath of office. One of the most important of all of the bases of a president's power is his political authority and his potential for extended political authority in the future. A president whose term was limited to one six-year stretch would be a president who could command about two years of enthusiasm, two years of acquiescence, and two years of obstruction.

There is already an eight-year limitation upon the tenure of a president—the act of the vengeful, Republican Eightieth Congress determined to punish the wraith of the four-term winner, Franklin D. Roosevelt. But this amendment to the Constitution has only had relevance to one president since its adoption—ironically to the Republican President Dwight D. Eisenhower. President Truman, who was specifically exempted from its provisions, refused to run in 1952. President Kennedy was assassinated before he had completed his first term, and President Johnson declined to run for a second full term.

President Eisenhower, of course, finished his second term with just about the same high degree of popular esteem that had marked his inauguration in 1953. But since he had been a president who preferred to preside rather than to rule, the degree of popular support he enjoyed is not relevant to the problem. He was not a man who sought to manipulate the instruments of political power, and therefore there is no way of measuring the effect of the two-term limitation upon his authority.

The case of Lyndon Johnson, however, is very much to the point. The erosion of his power became apparent within weeks after his announcement that he was withdrawing himself from contention in March of 1968. The last ten months of his administration were marked by frustration on every issue, with the sole exception of the convening of the Paris conference to discuss ways and means of ending the Vietnam War. Even here, while he succeeded in launching the conference it is impossible to avoid the clear implication that the Vietnamese participants, both North and South, stalled substantive discussions while they awaited the outcome of the November elections. Obviously, they wanted to take the measure of the incoming president before settling down to a genuine give and take at the bargaining table.

On every other issue, President Johnson was unable to command even a respectful hearing. One of the outstanding examples was the nuclear nonproliferation treaty, which enjoyed widespread support from leading members of both political parties. It was difficult to find an argument against the agreement, but the Republican presidential candidate, Richard M. Nixon, said that in his judgment Senate consideration should be postponed. The ostensible excuse was the invasion of Czechoslovakia by the Soviet Union late in the summer of 1968—an action which had serious implications in terms of world peace but very little relevance to the treaty. A more likely and obvious reason was that Mr. Nixon preferred to have the document ratified in his, rather than in Mr. Johnson's, administration. And members of Congress are notoriously quicker to react to a potential, as opposed to a lame-duck, president.

Far more humiliating, because it involved personal relationships, was the Senate's refusal to confirm the president's friend, Abe Fortas, as chief justice of the Supreme Court. Among grounds cited were a number of occasions upon which Mr. Fortas, while a justice, had given the president personal advice. Translated into political English, this was merely another way of saying that he was a friend to a president who would not be in office much longer. It was enough. The nomination was withdrawn to prevent defeat.

During the closing days of his administration, Mr. Johnson might well have recalled an episode in 1956 when, while still a senator, he challenged Governor Allen Shivers for control of the Texas delegation to the Democratic national convention. Mr. Shivers was a man of tremendous power. He had succeeded in 1952 in swinging Texas to Dwight D. Eisenhower and he had broken the two-term gubernatorial tradition which up to that point had governed the political life of the Lone Star State. He had encountered some bad troubles through scandals arising in his administration, but the scandals were not directly traceable to him and his conservative political viewpoint was unquestionably the viewpoint of Texas. He was handsome, articulate, and forceful. He had only one real weakness—he had declined to run for re-election in 1956 and was serving as a "lame-duck" governor.

John Connally managed the Lyndon Johnson campaign to control the Democratic delegation. He called every influential citizen of Texas, many of whom had a

long record of supporting Allen Shivers and opposing Lyndon Johnson. Connally had one message which he repeated over and over again: "Do you want to be with a
dead governor or a live senator?"

Allen Shivers suffered one of the most complete
defeats of any prominent political character in all of Texas
history.

Far more serious, however, would be the impact of a
one-term limitation upon the president in terms of his life-
lines to reality. It would be clear to him from the first day
in office that there was nothing political to be gained by
placating pressure groups in society. He would, therefore,
feel a far greater degree of freedom in following his own
desires and ignoring those groups within the nation that
displeased him.

It is, of course, a well-established tenet of American
mythology that it is virtuous for a political leader to be
"above" pressure groups. Every reformer pays lip service
to this concept (as long as political leaders are not "above"
the reformer's pressures). The puerility of this idea is ap-
palling. Obviously, a president should act along those lines
he believes to be right. But he should also act with political
skills which enable him to convince all groups in a society
that they are getting a fair shake. To assume that he will
be a "better" president because he does not have to listen
to constituent groups is to assume that democracy would
be a better system if it weren't so democratic.

It is a very simple matter to become impatient with
large groups of people who refuse to accept the wisdom of
a course followed by a political leader. Most politicians
manage to temper their impatience because they are looking forward to another test of their leadership at the polls.
No useful purpose can be served by establishing a system

which encourages the development of impatience into arrogance.

The concept that there are policies and programs which are immutably correct has been one of the most troublesome in the history of human government. It is especially troublesome in the modern age, which is dominated by "experts" who can bring to many problems knowledge and skills which undoubtedly supply answers. A businessman whose industry is sick has become accustomed to calling in market analysts, production engineers, cost surveyors, or management consultants. He sees with his own eyes that these technicians obtain results that are immediately demonstrable in terms of the profit-and-loss statement. The citizen who is ill is sent by his family doctor to a series of medical specialists who have divided up the human body and made specific areas their exclusive domains. Again the results are usually observable in terms of better health or at least a prolonged existence. The party organization which finds its treasury depleted is accustomed to calling in fund-raising experts who bring a wealth of knowledge to the gentle art of persuading citizens to part with a portion of their bank account for a worthy cause. Again, results are obtained which are immediately apparent and which can be set forth in terms of cold, hard figures that cannot be disputed.

It would be strange if this kind of atmosphere did not encourage the belief that there are government "experts" who can solve all the problems of the nation by combining elementary principles of qualitative analyses with electronic computers that bat out the correct answers in the twinkling of an eye. Of course, there are government "experts" who understand with considerable precision exactly how government works. There are men who can predict the course of a bill through Congress; who can plot the vagaries of the budget through a fiscal year; who can devise valid manpower charts. The problem, however, is that the experts can only answer the question of how decisions can be carried out. The basic problem of the decisions themselves remains and this is not a valid field for the bureaucrat.

The process of political leadership is far more than the mere charting of policies and programs. It is also the proper weighing of the resources that are available to meet those goals. Some of those resources can be judged with relative ease—finances, manpower, production capacity, raw materials. But the most important can be measured only through the intuition of the political leader —and that is the willingness of the people to support the actions that the political leader considers necessary. It does not matter what a president wants to do if the people are unwilling to do it. A political leader who ignores the popular will is not a hero but merely a shoddy craftsman who is not entitled to his job.

The type of political leader who rises to the heights of a Jefferson or a Lincoln or a Franklin Roosevelt does not, naturally, merely bow to the popular will and allow himself to be swept along by the currents. This is not political leadership in any sense of the word. But if he is unaware of those currents, he will be unable to pilot the ship of state to a safe harbor. He will not truly be leading.

No proposal which tends to separate a president from the political pressures of his constituency can possibly improve the operations of the presidency. All it will do is tend to make him an ineffectual voice issuing orders and decrees which serve as an irritant to inflame further the forces of disintegration that are always present in a society no matter how well ordered or how well planned it may be.

The proposal that House members serve a four-year term and be elected concurrently with the president would, at least, achieve the objective sought by its proponents. There is little doubt that it would make Congress more receptive to presidential desires. But this begs the question. Do we really advance the national interest by relieving the chief executive of this worry?

The mere fact that dealing with Congress is a worrisome proposition is probably the greatest value that body offers to the nation. A president who is anxious to secure enactment of his programs must walk carefully lest he tread on the sensitive toes of the men at the other end of Pennsylvania Avenue. He must (at least after the first fine flush of his inauguration has evaporated) listen to their opinions with some respect. He must take into account their problems if he is to secure the funds that he needs to manage the government. He must make strong efforts to build up a following on Capitol Hill and this he can only do through persuasiveness and compromise.

The Congress is one of the most sensitive barometers of public opinion available to the chief executive. The barometer may tell him some unpleasant things—but this is the function of a barometer. When a storm is approaching, a sea captain who refuses to consider the warning signs is a man who is doomed to lose his ship. Of course, the captain can go down with his ship, which may assure him a place in history, but it is not very comforting to the crew and their families, who are dependent upon his skill and judgment to survive.

Truly philosophical presidents who understood the nature of the problems of the office would welcome the midterm election regardless of its outcome. This is one of the few opportunities they have during the course of their administration of taking a sounding of the American people that is far superior to any readings that may be obtained by Dr. Gallup or Mr. Harris. The terms "philosopher" and "president" may be mutually exclusive, but this is no reason for the American people to indulge in the folly of depriving the president of one of his most valuable assets.

The antagonism felt by presidents toward Congress is entirely understandable. It arises out of the frustrations that inevitably come to any man who must grapple with the largely insoluble problems of a messy world and who must deal with the stubborn unreason of people in the mass. The legislative branch affords a convenient outlet for blowing off steam, though it is not very prudent to use it.

No president can admit, even to himself, that his problems stem from his inability to persuade the people of the rightness of his programs. In the United States, every politician must make due obeisance to the collective wisdom of the populace. Therefore, when a president's designs are frustrated, he must demonstrate, at least to his own satisfaction, that the popular will was with him but was somehow diverted or distorted by the machinery of government. The most satisfying method of achieving this rationalization psychologically is to zero in on the Congress.

Thus, Woodrow Wilson castigated the "little group of willful men" in the Senate who, he believed, had wrecked his grand design for world peace through American participation in the League of Nations. In the light of subsequent events, Wilson may have been right in his predictions of dire consequences should our country refuse to enter the League, although calamity and catastrophe are so much a normal condition of humanity that I am very skeptical of any claim that disaster resulted from a failure to do any particular thing. An objective student of the period, though, must admit that the voters simply were not ready for the step at the time. It was the American people—not the Senate—who frustrated the president.

Harry S Truman managed a successful election campaign by railing against the "do-nothing, good-for-nothing" Eightieth Congress. It was an effective tactic. But the Eighty-first Congress, which was elected with him, enacted virtually none of the bills Mr. Truman desired. Again, it was the American people, not the Congress, who frustrated the president.

None of this is to be construed as reflecting a belief that Congress is always right. Congress can be "wrong" just as the people can be "wrong"—overwhelmingly. Democracy does not seek to guarantee people wise and prudent government. Its real objective is to give them a voice in the management of their own affairs. Efforts to achieve that goal of necessity create tensions that focus upon the Congress more than any other governmental body. And those tensions can be eased only to the extent that we are willing to abandon our freedoms.

The proposal of a four-year term for House members has received short shrift from Congress thus far. That is what it deserves.

Neither this chapter nor this book will make any attempt to summarize or analyze all the proposals that have been advanced to "reform" or "strengthen" the presidency in recent years. There is a large body of academic literature on the subject, much of it excellent and with much of which I agree. This chapter merely singles out the few proposals that have been the subject of public debate on a reasonably large scale.

It is interesting that the only proposal which would seek to make the presidency *more*, rather than less, responsive to the people comes from outside the White House. It is the recommendation for direct national primaries to replace conventions as the device for selecting candidates. Generally, this idea is sponsored by those whose candidates have lost in the past few Democratic conventions.

This should not be confused with the drive for a direct election of the president. The latter is designed to eliminate the chance of a chief executive coming to office with only a minority of the people behind him. The possibility arises out of the existence of the Electoral College, a constitutional device which had validity in the early part of our history but which has little relevance to modern conditions. Abolition of the College, or at least of its power to frustrate the popular will, would be greeted with considerable relief but it would make little or no change in the conduct of the office of the presidency.

Direct presidential primaries, however, would make a difference because they would change the conditions under which the candidates are selected. Therefore, it is necessary to analyze this proposal, particularly since I do not think it wise, although it does meet the test of greater responsiveness.

In the first place nobody really can know what a national primary would do. The only experience so far with primaries has consisted of the presidential contests that are held in roughly a quarter of our states. It is folly to assume that the results would be identical if these primaries were extended to all fifty states. There is, however, a much deeper objection. Fundamentally, the workability of democracy rests upon a willingness of people to accept their second and third choices when they discover that they cannot get their first. For this reason, almost every facet of American government provides machinery for working out a consensus. In terms of the selection of a candidate, the national convention is the forum in which this is done.

The problem with the national primary is that it would deprive the voters of any mechanism through which the second and third choices could come into play. A vote is a "sudden-death" proposition that stops all further negotiation or conciliation. It is the "end of the line" and presents the choices in a simple "yes or no" form.

The problem here is easily illustrated. It is entirely possible that nationwide primaries could be settled by votes of 51 percent to 49 percent. The 49 percent would either have to capitulate to the will of the majority or walk out. In election years, however, there are not very many cases where people are willing to capitulate to the machinery. If they cannot get what they want, they are willing to bargain for a second choice on the thesis that they still have a share in the process. But a 51–49 situation—with no possibility of appeal—permits no second choices. The result would sooner or later be a party split and a proliferation of political sects that would bring the American government under its present structure to a halt because there is no machinery for forming a coalition government.

There is no guarantee that the bargaining process will automatically produce a great man. It resulted, in 1920, in the selection of Warren G. Harding as the Republican presidential candidate over a number of men who, by all contemporary accounts, were his superiors. But in the realm of politics, one must deal with relative concepts rather than with absolutes. Harding at least had the virtue of winning the election for the Republican party (Republican professionals would regard it as a virtue), and it turned out that for all of his inadequacies and for all the scandals that broke during his regime, he was very much in step with the national mood. His thinking pleased the public so much that his successor, who was elected without any difficulty, was merely a more careful and cautious carbon copy.

The bargaining process, moreover, frequently brings to the forefront men of stature who otherwise would have been unnoticed. The outstanding example in recent political history was that of Adlai Stevenson at the Democratic convention in 1952.

For the Democrats, 1952 was a year of tremendous difficulty. The combination of the Korean War, a series of petty scandals in President Truman's administration, and a heightening of tensions within the nation over the racial issue threatened to tear the party to pieces. There was no cohesive force in evidence other than a loosely defined coalition of "old New Dealers" like James Farley and congressional leaders like House Speaker Sam Rayburn. Important segments of the party in California and in the large urban centers were openly discussing the possibility of a split and obviously regarding the possibility with considerable equanimity. Only two candidates came to the convention with any real strength—Estes Kefauver of Tennessee and Richard B. Russell of Georgia. There were enough minor candidates (such as Senator Robert S. Kerr of Oklahoma and New York Governor Averell Harriman) to prevent either of the two leaders from securing the necessary two-thirds majority.

The nomination of either Senator Kefauver or Senator Russell would certainly have meant a party split of serious proportions. Kefauver was seen as a "liberal"—but a liberal with an abrasive personality who commanded a fanatical following and evoked a fanatical opposition. Russell was "the Dixie candidate" and, though highly respected and esteemed throughout the nation for his unquestioned intellectual capacity, totally unacceptable outside the South to a party which had dedicated itself to the cause of civil rights and which was heavily dependent upon the Negro vote in large Northern cities. It was inconceivable that any of the minor candidates could enlarge their support and capture the nomination.

Adlai Stevenson, the governor of Illinois, had taken himself out of the running several months earlier, but a small group of amateurs refused to accept his withdrawal and had opened a suite in the basement of the Chicago Hilton Hotel as a campaign headquarters. The professionals—Rayburn, Farley, and the then virtually unknown Lyndon B. Johnson—came to the conclusion that Stevenson would be the answer to the dilemma. He had unquestioned credentials as a liberal but lacked the abrasive personality that made Kefauver unacceptable. He had not been involved in any of the state presidential preference primaries and thus had not accumulated any enemies. He was a man of great eloquence and would have little difficulty in projecting his image to the public.

The Stevenson nomination, although a last-minute improvisation, was entirely due to the machinations of the "professionals." But from the moment of his acceptance speech, the Democratic party found itself involved in a love affair with its candidate.

Both Kefauver and Russell (the former somewhat glumly and the latter joyously) pledged their full support. Intellectuals throbbed to a man who could speak in an English uncluttered by clichés, and party professionals found that they could campaign for him without apologizing to their constituents. Stevenson, of course, lost the election but no one with a cool head thought that anyone could beat the Republican candidate, Dwight D. Eisenhower, in 1952. He did succeed in holding the Democratic party together, giving it a sense of purpose, and acting as a source of inspiration to party leaders until his death many years later.

It should be noted at this point that Adlai Stevenson was not, strictly speaking, an ideologue. He was a pragmatic man who refused to be bound by the formal structure of any political philosophy. In this, he was in perfect step with the mainstream of American politics, thus offering proof that a leader need not be sectarian or overly ideological to capture the imagination of millions of people.

The American system is simply not adapted to a multiplicity of ideological parties. It is possible in a parliamentary government to sustain as many parties as there are philosophies, but this possibility exists solely because the people under such a system do not elect their administrative leaders. Instead, they elect representatives of their own particular philosophy to a parliamentary body and these representatives work out the details of selecting the men who will actually manage the affairs of a nation.

This, of course, often results in a coalition. There are far too many different points of view among human beings for any one point of view ever to command a true and lasting majority. Somehow, representatives of those points of view must get together and work out the minimum basis upon which the administration is possible.

As the American people elect their chief executive directly, coalition at the government level is excluded. The final choice of a president is a "sudden-death" proposition. The Electoral College is not a body adapted to the type of bargaining that can go on in a parliament. Therefore, the coalescing forces in the American political system must exist at the party level rather than at the governmental level, and our two parties are actually coalitions rather than ideological choices.

A national primary would remove from the public scene the one part of our political process that permits bargaining between the second and third choices. With this bargaining point removed, it is impossible to imagine the government of this nation retaining any degree of tranquillity or stability. Every president would enter office with large parts of the population dead set against him and unwilling to be reconciled.

In summing up all the proposals to "reform" the presidency, they all fall on the same proposition. They fail to recognize the fundamental facts of the power relationships that have been created in our society. Some of them might tend to make the operations of the presidency more efficient, but nothing would be gained by increasing the effectiveness of operations that might be moving a society in the wrong direction. The art of politics remains the art of reconciling power relationships to the needs of a society. Any approach on any other premise is further doomed to failure.

There is more—much more—to the presidency than the kind of authority enjoyed by a production manager or a battalion commander. A president must be able to *lead* as well as to give orders. Proposals that seek to sustain his authority after he has lost his popular following are doomed to failure unless the proponents are willing to go to a police state. Rather than trying to cushion the White House against popular storms, efforts should be bent toward sharpening the president's political senses so that he can offer the only kind of leadership that is tolerable in a democracy.

★

One of the most profound changes that has come to the presidency has resulted from a new factor in American life—assassination as a political instrument. It is not that assassination itself is new—three presidents were killed before John F. Kennedy—but that it has become a continuous presence that seems to be lurking behind every shadow.

In the past, it was incomprehensible to most Americans that assassination could become an everyday fear. It seemed to be a remote horror, distant even from the violence that was such an integral part of frontier life. For at least two generations, it was merely a part of "history," something that belonged in the same category as the murder of the two princes in the tower or the killing of Julius Caesar.

Whatever may have been the reaction at the time, the assassination of Abraham Lincoln appeared to many in the perspective of history to be almost an appropriate climax to the life of a great and tragic man. President Garfield's administration made so little impact on the overall stream of American consciousness that today he is known to most of our people only because he was killed—and nine out of ten in any gathering of reasonably well-educated Americans would be hard pressed to name the assassin. It was not until the death of William McKinley that specific steps were taken against the American equivalent of regicide and the full-time job of protecting the president was assigned to the Secret Service.

In retrospect, it is strange that there have not been more attempted assassinations in American history. The office of the presidency is certainly one of the most tempting targets to twisted minds that has ever been established. To kill a president is to kill a nation and thereby reserve space in the halls of immortality—or at least ensure a permanent footnote in histories of the American republic. And, until World War I, the president was a highly accessible man. Carl Sandburg has a number of references to the manner in which Lincoln would encounter people with whom he did not have an appointment just on a stroll through the White House. Apparently, it was an open institution with nothing sealed off except the family living quarters.

It is not an open institution now. Access is possible only upon the basis of passes or appointments, with strict identification required both at the gate and inside the building. The tourists who throng the ceremonial part of the Mansion do so under the watchful eyes of guards who are as vigilant as they are pleasant. Every list of people invited to White House ceremonies or social affairs is carefully scanned and checked against government security files.

The careful control of entry to the White House, however, is not the process which has made such an important impact on the presidency. It would be necessary under any circumstances. Otherwise the building would be so filled with visitors that work in it would become impossible. The more important aspect is the determined effort of all concerned to make the security arrangements of the White House portable—to wrap them around the president whenever he ventures outside the grounds.

Harry S Truman was stretching things somewhat when he said that the Secret Service agent was the only man who could tell the president what to do. This is a type of hyperbole in which presidents, for some reason, glory (Lyndon Johnson was fond of telling everyone how his cook told him what to eat). But once the objectives of a presidential movement are set, the Secret Service pretty well has the last word on how the movement will be made, and for a group of men who are possessed of an unusually high degree of tact, they can be remarkably firm.

The rules are reasonably simple. Make trips as fast as possible. Avoid crowds wherever possible. Where crowds cannot be avoided (or where the president insists upon them), have the people gathered where they can be controlled. Command every high platform. Stand ready at every moment to get between the president and anyone who might pose a threat.

During the 1964 campaign, these rules—except for the last one—largely went by the board. Lyndon B. Johnson, whose love for crowds is insatiable, insisted on "pressing the flesh" at almost every street corner where more than three people were assembled. Perspiring Secret Service agents looked on in dismay as he plunged recklessly into vast throngs and stood on the top of his automobile to address the multitudes through a bullhorn—a perfect target for a sniper.

It is doubtful whether we will see his like again. In

the early months of 1968, before he withdrew from the field, worried assistants were fretting over the problem of how to campaign. It was unthinkable that he expose himself as he had in 1964 in view of the changed temper of the country. And he was not a good TV personality, probably because he was too self-conscious before the cameras and too determined to make a presentation instead of a communion with his fellow Americans.

Unless there is an extraordinary shift in the degree of national stability, an important factor has left American political life—the personal presidential campaign. It is difficult to picture any president ever again campaigning from the rear platform of a train, walking through huge street crowds gathered under tall buildings, shaking hands at outdoor rallies. The assassination of Robert F. Kennedy has made it clear that such activities involve unacceptable risks even when the candidate is a challenger and not currently holding the office.

The personal campaign is not to be despised, despite its carnival air and the mindless character of the slogans and political speeches. As an educational device, it left something to be desired—but the American people did learn something from it. It gave voters an opportunity to observe a man under conditions of stress and excitement where he would be unguarded in his reactions and his comments. Some of the judgments made under those circumstances were exceptionally shrewd. A man really cannot play a role for week after week of grueling travel. Sooner or later he will reveal his true character.

Even more important, however, it represented a form of communion between a leader and his people, a communion that was a two-way street. Voters who could see a man in person, perhaps even, with a little luck, get to touch him, somehow felt that they shared in the processes that governed them. Candidates, on the other hand, received a sense of drawing strength from the great mass.

Presidents and candidates for the presidency will, of course, continue to campaign, and science and technology has placed in their hands an instrument that solves the problem of security—television. Here is a device which can be perfectly controlled; which can be set up, if desired, in a bombproof room; which requires so few people in the president's immediate vicinity that everyone can be checked and cross-checked to the complete satisfaction of the most cautious security officer; and which, finally, can enable a president to reach an audience running into nine figures.

From every standpoint it seems ideal. The lighting can be controlled to present the candidate in the most flattering manner; camera angles can be dictated to show what he considers most photogenic; TelePrompTers can unroll his script in the most readable form; and no other media can bring a message to so many people at such a low cost per unit.

Of course there are problems. Some politicians are not adapted to television, probably because they take it so seriously. Others, like John F. Kennedy, find it ideal for their purposes—probably because he approached the technical process with an attitude of detached amusement. Further, it is dangerous to preempt a program beloved by millions of Americans, and almost impossible to find good air time that does not preempt something in that category.

But these are all problems of practice and management. The much more vital factor is that another barrier has been placed between the president and the people. One more link to reality has been snapped.

The medium that replaces the face-to-face campaign is a most peculiar one. It deserves a closer look. Television is at one and the same time the most personal and the most impersonal method of communication that has ever been contrived. It can bring a man into the living room, warm and vibrant, as a living presence. One hour later the same man can be watching himself on a replay with the detachment of a critic reviewing a theatrical performance. He can even write notes (and frequently does) directing himself on fine points that will improve his performance the next time around.

There are very few men who can literally stand outside themselves and criticize their own performance without suffering some confusion in their own identity. Unlike the old-time newsreel, which was shown under technical conditions that never permitted the viewer to forget that it was a mechanical device, television creates an illusion of immediate reality even though nothing is happening except the unreeling of magnetized tape through a series of spools. Even the screen upon which the pictures are flashed is encased in a cabinet designed to blend into the surroundings.

A man (not every man) who is viewing his own performance as it actually happened can easily slide into a feeling of divinity, convinced that he possesses godlike powers to change his identity—to become a Winston Churchill or a Franklin D. Roosevelt or an Abraham Lincoln, if only he can find the right speech writers, voice coaches, and makeup artists. The feeling comes much more easily to a man of strong ego living under circumstances where all his personal desires are indulged. Most presidents are in that category.

To the actor, of course, this is not a problem, as his

whole life consciously centers on the presentation of personalities other than his own. But a political leader, in order to carry out his functions, must have a number of aims of which making a presentation is only one, however important. In the age of television there is a strong temptation to subordinate all other priorities to the performance in a theatrical sense.

The preoccupation of presidents with television has increased as the years have gone by since its introduction on a large scale. Eisenhower brought Robert Montgomery into the White House as a coach and a "consultant." Kennedy made the transition to the live, televised press conference. Johnson installed a television studio in the White House and when he traveled always took along his own TelePrompTers and TelePrompTer crew. Nixon's aides chatter almost incessantly about the presidential "image," as built on TV with painstaking care.

Most of these developments parallel the spread of television as the principal medium of communication in the United States—a potent force that cannot be ignored. But a great deal of the obsessive discussion in the White House goes far beyond the actual impact of electronics upon the public. A large share arises out of the preemptive nature of the medium itself, the tendency of TV to set both the location and the timetable for an important event.

The cameras are big and clumsy. They take time to set up and even more time to check out. They raise questions of lighting, makeup, voice levels, background scenery. Above all, air time is precious and must be divided into fractions of minutes. All this means that it is usually easier to bring the story to the medium rather than the medium to the story.

Perhaps the epitome of this situation can be found in

the successful efforts of the Johnson administration to persuade the Congress to accept the State of the Union message
at nine o'clock in the evening rather than at the traditional
noon session. This put the event in prime viewing time,
although it is doubtful whether it actually secured a
larger audience since the hour eliminated coverage on the
major news shows between 6 and 7 P.M. Whether good or
bad from a public-relations standpoint, however, it demonstrated the capacity of television to override the established habits of two major branches of the government.

The most graphic illustration of the effects of TV upon
our government can be found in the White House press
conference. When televised, this has become as spontane-
ous as a Javanese temple dance but without the grace
which makes the latter such a deeply moving experience.
The realities are at their starkest when the conference is
held in the East Wing, where facilities are generally lacking
and must be improvised.

The reporters—in this instance supporting players
rather than information seekers—are brought in early to
pick their way to a seat through the maze of cords and
cables that litter the floor. Their roles are perfectly well understood. They are batting-practice pitchers, present to
serve the ball up over the plate where the hitter can take a
healthy swing. It is accepted practice that the first two questions will be allotted to the wire-service men, and that the
traditional "thank you, Mr. President" will be uttered by
the senior wire-service man.

The show—and that is what it is—must start on time.
The president enters the room upon receiving a cue from
the chairman of the television and radio pool (a post that
rotates with regularity) designed to put him on camera at
the hour or the half hour. He mounts the dais, asks the

correspondents to be seated, and proceeds with his announcements. He then opens himself to questions, with due obeisance, of course, to the wire-service understandings which have been cited previously.

The trappings are impressive although not very aesthetic. On either side of the president (but out of the lens angles) are signal corps men with "shotgun" microphones which they point at each correspondent who is recognized. Overhead is a rack designed to give him precisely the lighting he wants. The microphone into which he speaks is fed into a "mult"—a device which permits all the networks to pick up his voice without the necessity of mounting a microphone on the podium—which is also controlled by the signal corps.

There are rarely more than twenty questions, and only one to a correspondent. They are not controlled, although this has been tried with disastrous results on one or two occasions, simply because controls are not necessary. The president dominates the scene completely. The lead questions are easily predictable. The "follow-up" questions—the kind that narrow down generalizations or pinpoint evasions—are nearly impossible in a situation where 200 to 400 correspondents are clamoring for recognition and where time is limited. Any president who has done his homework will emerge unscathed, with a generality for the "tough" questions and a rebuff for the "impertinent" questions. It is a breeze.

For President Kennedy, who enjoyed the whole process hugely, it was a plus performance from which he emerged points ahead every time. This was to be expected. Interestingly enough, however, President Johnson, who dreaded the televised news conference, also ended each session with a distinct improvement in his "public image."

The cards are so stacked in favor of the White House that it does not really take professional skill to win.

Televised press conferences, with rare exceptions, are cut off ruthlessly in thirty minutes—a few less, if possible. The networks lose enough money by devoting a half hour to a "public service" program. It would really be mean to take them over that half hour where they would not only lose more money but would be faced with the problem of improvising some kind of a presentation once a scheduled show had been ruined by an unexpected presidential pre-emption of a crucial segment of time.

Occasionally an off-beat question will pop up, usually from a correspondent for a small newspaper. The president might receive an unexpected query about his views on the ultimate nature of life; his attitude toward equal rights for women; or his reaction to proposals to make the turkey the national bird. Rarely does the off-beat question bear upon important issues that are giving a president trouble. If he is witty, he can pick up some mileage with a quick response. If he is not, he can be noncommittal and no one will be hurt.

The obvious question that arises is the point of the whole exercise. It does give the people an opportunity to hear their president discuss basic issues of the day, but the discussion would vary little if he merely appeared and read a series of statements without the presence of news-papermen as "props." That is all the performance can possibly amount to so long as time is limited and so many correspondents are seeking recognition.

Democracy, of course, requires rituals as much as any other form of government and the televised news conference serves this purpose. It is at least equal—and probably superior—to the parliamentary question, which must be submitted in advance and which cannot take as many forms. But this is not the issue at stake. The salient point is that in a process which purports to be the supreme form of communication between a president and his people, the presentation has become the dominant factor. Performance, in a theatrical sense, rides roughshod over content. For all the public learns about a chief executive's thinking, the newsmen might as well sit in the front lobby and dutifully file the press releases handed out by the press office.

None of this is to imply that we live in an age of political salesmen in contrast to a remote past in which our leaders were "statesmen." Throughout history, every politician has resorted to every device available to "sell" himself to his constituency. The difference now is that the politician has nothing to pull him down to earth except the Nielsen ratings, and those will always be good where a president is concerned. The whole process is a performance, with a star who is also the producer and director and who is not going to let himself be upstaged. He can "project" his image with no more fear of face-to-face hostile reaction than the Queen of England when she makes a speech from the throne.

But no one in the modern world expects a queen or a king to actually run a government. There is almost universal agreement that a throne is an excellent platform from which to reign but an impossible platform from which to rule. It is far too comfortable, far too insulated from the harsh realities, to harden a man against the exigencies of statecraft.

What has really happened is that a device universally hailed as a boon to communication has become a one-way street. It is a means by which a man can conduct a monologue *in* public and convince himself that he is conducting a dialogue *with* the public. Nothing can be more damaging to the psyche of an individual and whatever damages a president, damages the nation.

It may well be that every aspect of the presidency damages the psyche of the man who holds the office. It was conceived as an eminence—an area of unlimited authority, although within a limited sphere. As the power of the United States has increased, so has the responsibility of the president and so has his isolation. One does not deal in quite the same way with a man who can hurl the atomic bomb as one does with a man who can command only a couple of frigates or two or three regiments.

It is futile to study the problem of security and the problem of public communication in the hope that forms can be found which will meet the first requirement and not cancel out the second. The simple rule of thumb is that the degree of security increases with the degree of isolation from the public and the degree of communication increases with the degree of public contact. Security and communication are mutually exclusive and the problem is not resolved by electronics. The latter merely adds to the confusion.

It is possible, of course, to conceive of forms of government in which neither would be a problem. A prime minister is not as vulnerable to assassination as a president and he owes his position to a parliamentary body which he must face frequently and whose members must in turn communicate directly with the electorate. But there is a vast gap between conception and accomplishment. This is not a parliamentary form of government and there is no reason to believe it will become one.

All that can be said with validity is that forces arising in the second half of the twentieth century have acted to place an even greater gap between the president and the people. The degree of presidential responsiveness has been diminished, and one more degree of darkness has been added to the shadows that are creeping over the American presidency as we have known it.

XII | IT CAN HAPPEN

A highly irrational personality, who under other circumstances might be medically certifiable for treatment, could take over the White House and the event
never be known with any degree of assurance.

This statement is not based upon any pretensions to
psychiatric knowledge, and any psychiatric words in this
chapter are to be read in their popular sense. No effort will
be made—or should be made—to indulge in amateur medical diagnosis. But I do have some experience with the
reaction of human beings to irrational behavior, and it is
clear to me that where presidents are concerned, the tolerance level for irrationality extends almost to the point of
gibbering idiocy or delusions of identity.

To put it more simply, no one is going to act to inter-
fere with the presidential exercise of authority unless
the president drools in public or announces on television
that he is Alexander the Great. And even in these extreme
cases, action would be taken hesitantly indeed.

This reluctance, of course, does not spring merely
from awe of high office or fear of retaliation. At bottom, it
is a reflection of the ultimate nature of the presidential of-

fice—an environment in which for all practical purposes the standards of normal conduct are set by the president himself. To those immediately around him, he is the one who determines what is rational and what is irrational, and the public reaction to whatever he does is not immediate unless it brings on catastrophe.

Added to this is the protective screen the White House draws around its principal occupant. He is surrounded by assistants who consider their number-one goal in life to be that of presenting their "Chief" in the most favorable possible light. They have pipelines reaching into the vast federal bureaucracy comprising more than 2,500,000 people and they have the necessary levers to manipulate this machinery in order to achieve their goals—including the projection of a "positive" image. In any administration and under any circumstances, this bureaucracy may provide some sources for adverse stories in the press, but these stories come from an antiadministration "underground," usually left over from a preceding administration, which can never command quite the aura of credibility that surrounds even an unpopular president.

Finally, there is a widely accepted assumption (which is entirely valid) that a president lives under extraordinary pressures and must find extraordinary means of blowing off steam. A president will be forgiven for acts that would lead to the banishment from civilized society of almost any other human being—for blatant rudeness, for eccentric attire, for obsessive secrecy. Only a churl will "blow the whistle" on a man who is racked with the agony of facing daily the apocalyptic decisions of life and death which are almost routine in the White House, and the churls rarely carry weight with large segments of the population. It is virtually certain that the personal attacks upon Franklin

D. Roosevelt and his family by the conservative press were an asset from the standpoint of building popular sympathy. The American people thought that it just wasn't fair play.

Yet the fact remains that the problem of the unbalanced president is on the minds of every close observer of the political process. It is discussed in hushed tones—and the discussion becomes even more intense whenever a scientific or technological breakthrough produces some new and awe-inspiring weapon or some new method of eavesdropping upon the private life of another nation.

Although the implications are obvious, this is a matter that has been treated in literature almost entirely as a question of fiction. The best-known work is Fletcher Knebel's novel, *Night at Camp David*, which faced up to the issue squarely and explored the ramifications thoroughly. What Knebel discovered, and what every serious student of government has discovered, is that within the contemporary context there is no workable solution to the problem. In order to bring the book to an emotionally satisfying end, Knebel was forced to resort to the lame device of a presidential abdication in a moment of lucidity.

The issue, of course, does not arise out of the frothing-at-the-mouth or the "I am Napoleon" insanity which represents the popular stereotype of mental imbalance. Such manifestations are obviously incapacitating and easily handled under the recently enacted Twenty-fifth Amendment to the Constitution. The problem does arise out of the much more common phenomenon of erratic behavior which can still be presented to the world in a plausible form and which will not be recognized as irrational until disaster has resulted.

The framers of the Twenty-fifth Amendment stepped gingerly around this question. In private conversations, they admitted that it was their major motivation. On the record and for the legislative history, they contented themselves with devising language that applied only in the event of crippling or total disability.

A part of the language of the Twenty-fifth Amendment is worth quoting at this point:

> Whenever the Vice-President and a majority of either the principal officers of the Executive Departments or of such other body as Congress may by law provide transmit to the President *pro tempore* of the Senate and the Speaker of the House of Representatives a written declaration that the President is unable to discharge the powers and duties of this office, the Vice-President shall immediately assume the powers and duties of the office as Acting President.

This language was followed by an outline of complicated procedures through which the president would resume his duties once the disability had ceased. But the very complications of the procedure for resumption indicate the inadequacy of the machinery. On great questions of political policy, complicated procedures are rarely workable. Legislative draftsmen resort to them only when they are confronted with a problem for which they really do not have a satisfactory solution. In effect, when the Twenty-fifth Amendment is reduced to its simplest terms, it states that the president shall take up his duties once again when he *thinks* he is no longer disabled, and nothing can stop him from doing so except the objections of the vice-president and a majority of the cabinet backed by a two-thirds vote from both houses of Congress—a rather difficult force to assemble.

On two, and possibly three, occasions in our history, this kind of machinery might have been valuable. The

first involved the several weeks in which President Garfield vegetated in a comatose state that ended in death
after he was shot in 1881. The second was the long period
of almost total disability of President Woodrow Wilson after
he suffered a stroke in 1919. In neither case did the vice-
presidents assume any of the duties of the presidency, out
of fear that they would be accused of usurping the powers
of the office. To this day it is unclear who actually ran the
United States during those periods, although it is generally
assumed without proof that Mrs. Wilson exercised the presidential powers during the last year of her husband's term.
The consequences were not catastrophic simply because
humanity had not reached a stage of technological development in which men were capable of destroying life
on this planet. But no one can study the last year of Wilson's administration without concluding that the seeds of
serious trouble may have been planted during the time
when a vital man at the helm of government could have
been able to continue policies of international cooperation
that might have forestalled World War II.

The third occasion was far less serious in scope. It was
President Eisenhower's heart attack in 1955. No one but
his doctors will ever be certain of the extent of the disability suffered by the president. It is unlikely that it was very
great, as he was obviously a coherent, thinking man
throughout the period. But by 1955, the atomic bomb was
a major item in the arsenals of two great world powers and
humanity had arrived at a point in technology where total
destruction of life was at least a drawing-board possibility.
The president's illness forced political leaders at least to
face up to the possibility of total incapacity short of physio-
logical death, and the Twenty-fifth Amendment was the
result. It is interesting, however, to note that it took the

Congress ten years to submit a constitutional amendment to the states. Even under these extreme circumstances, no one wanted to admit that a president might "lose his marbles."

In the background of the discussion was another fear. It was simply that any machinery which permitted any group of men to deprive a president of his powers for any reason whatsoever could open the doors to a *coup d'état* by an ambitious vice-president who could mobilize a majority of the members of the cabinet. The *coup d'état* has been unlikely in the United States because of the long traditions of democracy, but that is no reason to place temptation in front of ambitious men.

The real difficulty is that irrational behavior is not necessarily illogical behavior. In fact, the finest logicians that the average person meets in the course of a lifetime are likely to be people that any psychiatrist would promptly label as neurotic personalities. Plausibility is virtually the hallmark of the nut and the crank. The man who believes that the world is flat can usually outargue his fellow citizen who knows that the world is spherical. The anti-Semite who ascribes all the evils of history to a Jewish conspiracy can marshal many more convincing arguments in support of *his* thesis than can be countered by the more balanced human being who knows that the *Protocols of the Elders of Zion* are sheer fantasy. And anyone who has ever made the mistake of arguing with a recently converted Marxist who has just traveled the road to Damascus has discovered that he simply cannot win. The "true believer"—neurotic or otherwise—always works harder than the "normal" person.

The problems of irrationality are complicated enough in ordinary everyday life. Most of us live in a world peopled by office troublemakers, guard-house lawyers, and neurotic relatives. Fortunately, most of them can cause only a minimum of trouble. But in the political world, the problem of the neurotic assumes proportions that are gigantic. Politics and neurosis are inextricably intermingled because the neurotic personality is usually more articulate and more logical in expressing stands on the great issues of the day. Politics probably would not exist at all without neurotic drives that compel men to exert leadership and extend their personalities to dominance over others. What keeps most political leaders from rushing headlong into catastrophe is the fact that their own neurotic drives must clash with the neurotic drives of others and in the conflict certain forms of social sanity are bound to emerge.

The presidential office, however, exists in an environment which is free of many of the restraints with which all other political leaders must contend. Face-to-face confrontations with opponents are rare and occur only at a time and place of the president's own choosing. He is obviously unlikely to select circumstances which are not to his advantage. When the president does confront his political enemies, he fires his salvos from a fortress—the White House. Here he is cushioned against all the hazards that must be faced by a politician in the field. The whole purpose of his physical environment is to cater to all his cravings—psychological as well as physical.

It is certain that whatever neurotic drives a president takes with him into the White House will be fostered and enhanced during his tenancy. He lives in a world that is the delight of the immature personality—a universe in which every temper tantrum is met by instant gratification of the desire which caused the tantrum. Nobody is going to say "no" to his little demands, and the "no's" that are said to the big demands come in the most diplomatic and tactful forms.

This is the condition which surrounds a man who has the power to order troops into battle; to decide the distribution of billions of dollars of the nation's wealth; and to use or withhold atomic weapons that can incinerate tens of millions of people in a matter of hours. The American system of government places in the hands of one man the responsibility for making decisions that require the utmost maturity and then surrounds him with an atmosphere that encourages the development of the most immature impulses.

The problem is compounded by the awareness of most people that their political leaders will be eccentric under any circumstances. Generally, Americans glory in the foibles of their presidents. Harry Truman's salty and sometimes explosive language was tut-tutted by prudish moralists, but for most Americans it established a bond of identification. Jack Kennedy's compulsive urge to play touch football delighted people who wished they could go through life like Peter Pan, without ever growing up. Lyndon Johnson's speed mania on the highways was a secret source of enjoyment to the millions of American males who would dearly love to roar down the roads subject to no check by highway patrolmen.

Neurotic behavior is merely eccentric behavior extended beyond the bounds within which it is merely amusing. Furthermore, who is to say what behavior is neurotic and what is merely eccentric? The entire history of psychiatry affords no workable guidepost in the field of political activity. Boiled down to essentials, neurotic behavior is manifested only by activity that does not conform to the standards and the structure of contemporary society, and what is "normal" in one age can be totally irrational in another. A fourteenth-century judge who believed that a man's guilt or innocence could be determined by forcing him to grasp a red-hot bar was evidencing rational behavior. He was expressing the considered wisdom of his age. But a twentieth-century judge who proposed such a test would be promptly locked in a padded cell. The juries who tried and executed witches in Salem, Massachusetts, were in perfect conformity with the "normal" behavior of the seventeenth century. Anyone who suggested at the time that "witchcraft" was a figment of the imagination would have been treated as a fit candidate for the nearest lunatic asylum. Today, a trial for witchcraft would be at best a curiosity (possibly staged by a district attorney seeking to clear the statute books of some obsolete laws) and more likely evidence that a community had lost its senses.

The political community, furthermore, does not, and cannot, rely upon empirical evidence as a guide to truth. The fundamental material with which it deals consists of the hopes and the fears of people. These hopes and fears always approximate some form of reality but the boundary lines are never clear. The danger is greater in the field of fear than it is in the field of hope because there are so many things in the world to fear that it is simple to interpret the whole universe in paranoiac terms. For example, there are Communist plots in just about every non-Communist nation in the world aimed at the overthrow of the existing government. To deny the existence of such plots is to commit an absurdity—to fly in the face of common sense. But the fact that there are Communist plots does not mean that all unorthodox activity or that all opposition to a government is based on Communist plots, or even that the Communist plots are of sufficient magnitude to present a real danger. Neurotic behavior can begin with a perfectly normal, sensible desire to preserve a government from those who would overthrow it. But who is there who can define the boundary between an illegitimate desire to overthrow a government and a legitimate desire to change it? Politicians, of course, must constantly make such assessments because it is essential to their activity that they correctly gauge the motivations of the opposition.

Since this is an age of tremendous faith in the validity of empirical science, the few proposals that have been made in this field assume that a board of psychiatrists could always be convened to pass upon the mental balance of a president. This idea is utterly impractical. In the first place, medical men are probably the least qualified of all professionals to pass judgment upon what political context is "normal" and what is "neurotic." They must spend far too much of their lives learning their highly complicated trade to absorb enough of the other intellectual disciplines. In the second place, however, what president who is in a coherent frame of mind would ever permit himself to submit to such a board? The question answers itself once we realize that coherence and plausibility are not imcompatible with neurotic behavior.

We return, therefore, to the only possible test that can be applied to any political leader. This is the judgment of his peers on his *political* behavior. This, of course, does not address itself to psychiatric questions. But it would, of necessity, include psychiatric questions even though not considered under that name.

An unbalanced president invariably engages in activity which repels his political colleagues and spurs them to some form of negative action. Because of the semisacrosanct position of the president,.this negative action cannot go so far as to remove him from office except under circumstances so extreme that the removal would be effected by revolution (or at least a *coup d'état*) if no legal machinery or impeachment were available. Consequently, people have a tendency to "put up" with irrational behavior on the part of a president. He can insult his closest friends, cut up his political allies and favor his political enemies, storm and rage over trifles. The worst that can happen to him is a muted grumbling and a steady erosion of confidence on the part of the people. Regardless of the grumbling and regardless of the erosion of confidence, the reins of power will stay in his hands. He will still have the authority to drop the atomic bomb on another nation even though in the privacy of Senate cloakrooms experienced men are whispering that "the president is nuts." And if anyone should raise the question in public and seek to initiate the constitutional process of impeachment or the processes of the Twenty-fifth Amendment, it would immediately become a political question, with strong suspicions on the part of the large segments of the public that a revolution is under way. Faced with this situation, responsible men would invariably conclude that it is wiser to put up with a president whose mental balance is suspect than to divide the country by a bitter debate over his removal.

Whatever the shortcomings of a parliamentary government, it does afford an answer to this problem. A prime minister can be removed from office by a vote of "no confidence" without any question ever being raised as to his mental or emotional capacity. As for the chief of state in a parliamentary system, his emotional stability is entirely irrelevant to the health of the governmental structure. He can give no orders, pass no judgments, control no funds. The only requirement is that his heart and his lungs func-

tion and that he be physically able to say the few words
that are necessary when he meets the chief of another state
or when he summons a new political leader to his official
residence to direct him to form a new government. It is, of
course, desirable that he be able to conduct himself with
dignity, but even this is not absolutely essential. In a parliamentary form of government, the chief of state can be
so surrounded by courtiers that any unpleasant idiosyn-
crasies will not be apparent.

It is obviously far too late for the United States to establish a parliamentary government on the lines of the
British system. Systems of government are created only by
a revolutionary act followed by a lengthy process of evolu-
tion. Therefore, men who are drawing up blueprints for
governmental organization without revolution had best be
certain that those blueprints fit the political realities of
the nation.

Nevertheless, it is apparent that no satisfactory solution can ever be found to the potential problem of the
mentally unstable president within the present framework.
So long as a man stands without peers at a summit of power,
he can be removed from office only by what amounts to a
coup d' état. Complicated machinery for psychological testing or for medical declarations of incompetency will not be
accepted by the American people—or for that matter any
other people—without arousing strong suspicions. Anyone
who has ever listened to conflicting psychiatric testimony
in a criminal proceeding will never be willing to accept a
technical verdict as to whether a man's psychic health is
sufficient for him to exercise the instruments of power.

Somehow, there must be a conversion of the operating
authority of the presidency to a managerial status—one in
which a president can be challenged without impugning

his sanity or his balance. The intuitive judgment of brother politicians, of course, is a vague standard which can never be defined with any precision. But ultimately, it represents the only method of solving a political problem and therefore it is the only direction in which there can be any hope.

★

While working on this book, I asked a professional political scientist whose opinions I respect highly to review some of the earlier chapters. I had planned to use these sections as the basis for a lecture at an Eastern university and wanted to test the concepts on someone experienced in speaking to academic audiences.

After a few days, he returned the manuscript to me with a number of suggestions (all of which I incorporated) and after a brief discussion of specific points he said: "But these are all minor. The big question you will face is what you propose to do about it. You can't get away with presenting a problem without a solution before an American audience."

Naturally, I had planned to present a solution. It had not seemed to me a matter of any great difficulty—and still does not seem very difficult provided that I am not troubled intellectually by a "solution" that will never go any farther than the paper upon which it is written. But my friend's words introduced a disturbing note. Obviously, what he was saying is that American audiences are conditioned to a political presentation formula in which a "proposal" must follow a "problem" just as a stage blackout must follow the scene in which the burlesque comedian squirts seltzer water on the chorine's panties. It is not that the thought becomes invalid if it lacks a solution (as a play becomes invalid if it lacks a denouement) but that it becomes unacceptable. It suddenly became apparent to me that there was a converse to this proposition—that some very flimsy thinking by both academic political scientists and professional politicians has been "validated" over the years simply because they presented a "proposal."

I thought back over the years to:

> The Texas congressman with a large Latin constituency who was applauded in the press annually for a set speech proposing that the United States double its appropriations for Latin America.

> The senator with presidential ambitions who barked at his speech writer: "God damn it! I want a proposal in every speech I make even if it's only to build a shed 18 by 11 by 10 in Rock Creek Park."

> The group of academic political scientists centered on the Library of Congress who resolved solemnly every year that American political parties should become "responsible" and be held to their platforms.

> The "laundry list" of legislative proposals that Harry S Truman sent to each incoming session of Congress—to the delight of progressive columnists and the wry amusement of the Capitol Hill hierarchy.

Originally, I had planned to work out a system of parliamentary government for America. It still looks good to me—on paper. It would call for the conversion of the House of Representatives into a parliamentary body empowered to select the managers of the nation's affairs, including a "chief of government." These managers would serve as long as they enjoyed the confidence of the parliament or until the parliament had completed a four-year term. Loss of confidence in those four years would present the chief of government with two options—ask the president (elected for a ten-year term) to dissolve the body and hold new elections, or resign and make room for the appointment of new managers.

This system would answer most of the problems that I have raised. It would enable the chief of government to concentrate on the affairs of the nation and place the functions of chief of state in the hands of a man who had no power. The chief of government would be answerable on a daily basis to the criticism of his colleagues, who would approach him in no awe of majesty. The country would not be stuck for a fixed term of years with a chief executive in whom the people had lost confidence. The power to remove the chief of government would not be exercised too irresponsibly because he would have the option of calling new elections, and no politician faces any more elections than are strictly necessary. Ideologically responsible parties would be encouraged because if they elected even a few members to the parliament, they would have some ability to influence the selection of members of the government.

Of course, what I have outlined leaves many problems to be resolved. What would happen to the Senate? What should be done to election districts? How should the Constitution be amended to eliminate the separation of legislative and executive but maintain the independence of the judiciary? I am not tackling these problems even though they would not be difficult to handle. I am leaving them alone because none of this is going to happen anyway or has even a chance of happening without a revolution. And I don't want to perpetrate another "blueprint" merely to make an analysis acceptable to the audience.

The American people are *not* going to call a constitutional convention to form a parliamentary government. They are *not* going to separate the functions of chief of government and chief of state. They are *not* going to undergo the subtle intricacies of rewriting a document that has served them since 1789. And if they *do* call a constitutional convention, it will probably be for the purpose of abolishing the Bill of Rights and restricting the authority of the judiciary.

Governments do not arise out of the blueprints of political thinkers any more than religions arise out of the systems constructed by theologians. Both are the products of ecstatic events—revolution in one case and revelation in the other. The technicians are called in after the fact to rationalize the actions of the revolutionaries or the prophets and to establish the institutions and liturgies that keep them in power.

In terms of what the American people will do *consciously* about the presidency in the next few years, the answer is very little. It is possible that the Constitution will be amended to eliminate the Electoral College—but this is hardly a basic change. It merely eliminates the freakish possibility of a minority president. And, while common sense calls for this step, it would not alter the environment in which the chief executive lives and works.

What will *happen* to the presidency, however, is something else. People do not have as much conscious control over their social destinies as they would like to believe. But there are evolutionary processes in society which make fundamental political changes and these are worth analyzing.

No view of the American scene at the present time affords any comfort to an observer, unless he is a hardened revolutionary. The dominant theme of our national life has become violence—so much so that a presidential commission has been established to study its causes, the third such commission bearing directly or indirectly on the subject in four years.

It is arrant nonsense to conclude that this condition is inherent in the social fabric of the United States—to say with H. Rap Brown that "violence is as American as cherry pie." It would be equally valid (and equally meaningless) to say that violence is as Mexican as frijoles, as German as weisswurst, as English as fish and chips, as French as croissants, or as Swedish as smorgasbord. Every society has gone through periods of savagery and no amount of ingenuity has succeeded in eliminating upheaval as a periodic factor in human affairs.

Generally speaking, violence characterizes two stages in national development. The first is during the formative years when there are very few customs or rules to govern social and economic conduct. The second is during a period of disintegration when institutions have lost their capacity to respond adequately to internal strains. The real question is not whether violence is a part of American life but which stage of violence is now upon us.

When Rap Brown compares tear gas, skull cracking, and city burning to cherry pie, he is actually attempting to be reassuring. In effect, he is saying that we have gone through all of this before—even in the recent past—and we have survived as a nation with our society and our government relatively intact and even in some respects improved. A plausible case can be made for this argument.

The frontier, which was with us until the fourth quarter of the last century, was a region of lawlessness where a man's ability to survive depended upon his strength and his ruthlessness. Yet today it serves as the source for a body of mythology with which virtually all Americans can identify.

Labor strife, in many respects as ferocious as the bloodletting of the Paris Commune, was still erupting less than forty years ago. Yet, organized labor today has become so respectable that it is difficult to distinguish a gathering of union chiefs from a meeting of the board of directors of a large corporation.

The New York draft riots of the 1860s, which were put down only by the threat of artillery in the streets, were as destructive of the city as the ghetto eruptions of the past few years. Yet, they were surmounted and the North went on to win the Civil War.

Impressive as these examples may be, however, they do not afford genuine parallels to what is happening to us now. All these events took place under circumstances where American institutions possessed flexibility, chiefly because they had not been in existence long enough to suffer hardening of the political arteries. It was possible to improvise responses with little regard to the constrictions that the past can impose upon the present—even in the case of the labor strife.

Furthermore, the instigators of past American violence were all people who had someplace to go. They were men and women who could see light at the end of the tunnel—who merely had to clear some obstacles out of the way to gain their place in the sun. This was true of the frontiersman, the craftsman, and the immigrant. They were able to approach the bloodletting with a sense of mission and an air of exuberance.

A look at the current American scene raises grave doubts that our present difficulties are similar in character. Let us begin with a few observations on the sources of American disarray.

Basically, there are two groups mounting a major challenge to our social structure and, interestingly enough, they come from opposite poles of the economic spectrum —the privileged elite and the poverty-stricken urban masses. The first group, of course, consists of our college students and the second of blacks living in slums.

At first glance, this appears to be an improbable combination, for the two groups are not acting in concert despite the best efforts of the more radicalized white youth to forge an alliance. The black militants want nothing to do with them. In addition, the professed goals differ widely —the whites concentrating on the war in Vietnam and the Negroes on political power for their own race.

There is, however, one common bond. Both groups are reacting to frustration, and while they may not be engaged in a common cause, they have, through their principal spokesmen, expressed an identical determination to tear the society apart if they do not get what they want. They have demonstrated convincingly that the threat is not an idle one.

It is of little avail to argue that the black militants and the student radicals are only a minority of Negroes and white youth. This is almost certainly true. But it does not alter the fact that large areas of some of our greatest cities have been left in ruins reminiscent of the bombing destruction of World War II, and that some of our greatest universities—revered objects in our society—have been disrupted and shut down for significant periods. There are social dynamics at work which can give minorities the power of a well-used battering ram.

The peril of the moment is heightened by the absence in our society of any consensus on methods of dealing with dissent. The professed demands of the student radicals and the black militants center on goals which are impossible to achieve. The students are challenging the concept of social organization itself and the blacks are demanding a status to which, in justice, they are entitled but which could exist only if the nation could go back 300 years and start over again without slavery.

In such times, only the most sensitive and subtle political leadership can possibly lead the people through turmoil without major bloodshed. The reaction from Washington thus far does not appear very reassuring.

In the Johnson administration, the major effort to placate youth was a public-relations effort to stress the youthful quality of the White House staff. Inspired stories appeared in magazine after magazine listing the aides who were under thirty, and the president himself in addressing a college group dwelt heavily on the fact that when they came to the White House they could deal with people near their own age.

The effort could hardly be called a success. Most of the "young" people in the White House were ambitious "Establishment" types (as could easily be anticipated) and impressed the student radicals as captives of the "power structure"—white Uncle Toms. About the only result was alienation of older people who received the impression that the president was not concerned with their problems.

The approach to Negro problems had a sounder base

and was more rationally conceived. Lyndon B. Johnson has a deep, sincere sympathy with black Americans, whom he felt were like himself in being born and reared in poverty (or, at least, under severe economic handicaps). The result was a stream of measures to train unskilled workers for useful employment, improve educational opportunities, open up jobs which previously had been labeled "white only," and clean up the intolerable conditions of the ghettos. Unfortunately, the efforts were too little and too poorly financed. They were also too late. The black revolution had passed the stage where progress would satisfy. The militants were interested only in revenge—revenge for the centuries in which they had had to accept humiliation as a condition of their daily lives.

The record of the Nixon administration has been blurred. He, too, has made a conscious effort to impress the public with the youthfulness of his staff. Otherwise, there is no definite indication as to how he proposes to deal with young people. Negro leaders are tending to the belief that they will be ignored completely.

In an extraordinarily large percentage of life's crises, it is a good rule that if you just close your eyes, they will go away. The difference between the "good" politician and the "inspired" politician is that the latter knows when his eyes *must* be open and when he *must* act. There is every reason to believe that the present crisis will not evaporate. If anything, it is reaching more deeply into key elements of our population.

Mr. Nixon undoubtedly gained considerable popularity by temporizing with his problems during his first few months in office. The great majority of Americans are tired of "action" and are in a mood to blame their current difficulties upon the hectic spurts of activity during the Johnson administration. But the Nixon popularity has been gained at a tremendous cost. Each passing day pins the crises more squarely upon him and diminishes his capacity to use his predecessor as a scapegoat.

This process applies with heavy force (and, it should be said, very unfairly) to his key problem—Vietnam. When Mr. Nixon took office, it was "Johnson's war," just as it had been, for a while, "McNamara's war." Now, as the days drag by, it is becoming "Nixon's war," and the public is not very likely to continue to accept the argument that he inherited it. Unfortunately, there is little he can do about the situation that he has not done already. In the early days of his administration, he might have emulated Charles de Gaulle and pulled out. Now he is committed to continue the negotiations, and the key to his future lies in the hands of men in North Vietnam who are unlikely to hand it to him except at a price which is now unacceptable.

A society confronted with insoluble problems usually turns to its organs of repression. This process is now under way. Its beginnings are apparent in municipal and state elections and in the rising "law-and-order" movement. The majority—which is neither black, young, nor poverty-stricken—is gathering its forces to lash back. The liberal movement is at an ebbtide and people just want some peace.

It is at this point that a key question comes to the fore-front. Are the organs of repression reliable as far as the "power structure" is concerned? The honest answer is one that is mixed and uncertain. The response must be—the police yes; the army probably but not for sure.

The various police forces throughout the nation have demonstrated already that they are willing to club down revolt by either radicals or blacks. They are groups of career men whose primary loyalties are to their leaders. Furthermore, where students are concerned they are confronting people for whom they feel an almost gut antipathy—a privileged elite that sees them as a lower order of human being and that makes no secret about its feelings.

The army, however, is a different proposition. The war in Vietnam has led to the drafting of enormous numbers of young men who do *not* regard the military life as an adequate career and who are subject to the same emotions and the same reactions that are moving young people on the "outside." In addition, efforts to escape conscription have brought into the ranks of the national guard and the organized reserves thousands of young people who are similarly inclined.

A conscript army is never a totally reliable force for the suppression of dissent. The business of maintaining internal order must be left to the professionals if the leaders of a nation are to feel secure. And the beginnings of disaffection are already apparent within the armed forces of the United States.

Thus far, the signs are meager and this country retains the capacity to throw first-class troops into battle in Vietnam, but the mere fact that the signs can exist at all is significant. Antiwar "coffee houses" near military posts, "underground" newspapers printed and circulated on army bases, lawsuits to enjoin the mobilization of organized reserve units may appear to be insignificant activities. Contrast the situation, however, with what would have happened had there been similar activity in the preceding two wars. There would have been a massive and savage retaliation by the entire community.

For the first time since the Civil War, the United States must give serious consideration to the possibility of military disaffection. This does not mean that revolt is seething among the troops or that they are anywhere near it. It does mean that seeds have been planted which can sprout with remarkable rapidity in the climate of modern civilization. There are now openly revolutionary forces at work within our country—forces that are having far more success than their Communist or anarchist predecessors.

The genius of the American system has been that up to this point, except for the Civil War, it has successfully avoided large-scale "confrontations" within our society. But present-day revolutionaries are deliberately developing confrontation techniques with a notable degree of success. They are alienating the majority, but they are radicalizing the youthful elite and the youthful blacks who occupy strategic positions in the center of our cities.

The question is raised: Can our political system cope with these strains? The answer is probably not. We are committed to a system which stresses stability simply because this was the most urgent need at the time it was devised. Now we are in a period which requires the utmost of flexibility—and that is a quality which is lacking.

It is possible, of course, that the Vietnam War will come to an end within a few months and a relatively lengthy period of peace will break out, but this eventuality is not under our control. We have no reason to believe that a cessation of slaughter in Southeast Asia will not be replaced by strains of a similar magnitude elsewhere. What has been demonstrated is that our form of government, which has stood virtually intact since 1789, is unable to withstand the stresses of the modern world.

It is a form which commits us to an administration for a fixed period of four years regardless of the public support accorded to the administration. It is a form of government which basically centers on one man and therefore does not allow adequate outlets for the aspirations of minorities. It is a form which isolates the man who holds the nation's highest office and shields him from reality.

Under the circumstances, change is inevitable. But no one can predict what form that change will take.

I am convinced it will not come through the cool type of intellectual exercise in which I indulged at the beginning of this chapter. Society does not work in that manner and never has. Even if it did, the forces that are compelling change would regard the structure of government as irrelevant to their demands. Many of their leaders regard government itself as irrelevant.

It is futile to reassure ourselves by repeating the shibboleth that today's radicals will be tomorrow's conservatives. This has been a truism in the past but it does not describe the process that is taking place today. The trend is for the replacement of radicals by militant radicals and then by more militant radicals. The "tired" radicals, who were so common in the 1940s and the '50s were basically men and women who had returned to childhood values against which they had rebelled. The revolutionaries of the 1960s—whether student or black militant—do not have such values to which they can return.

Again, we are faced with problems to which there is no good solution. The tragedy of humanity is its inner confidence that it can resolve all problems when the best it can do is to survive—and even that is in question.

The more probable outcome of our current difficulties will be a "man on horseback"—a George Wallace with a broader appeal or a Ronald Reagan with greater depth. It is certain that faced with a choice of chaos or suppression of dissent, most people will accept suppression of dissent. The human spirit cherishes freedom but the spirit is within men and women in varying degrees—and for most, stability has a higher priority.

The middle course between chaos and suppression of dissent, of course, is subtle and sensitive political leadership of the most pragmatic variety, leadership which balances delicately the factors of stability and freedom of expression. This is what we have had for nearly two centuries but it does not exist today. In this probably lies the twilight of the presidency. As an institution, its only hope for survival is to leave the museum where it operates and plunge into the world of reality; to walk the streets that real men and women walk; to breathe the air that real men and women breathe. The prospects are dim.

★

Conclusion

I must end by acknowledging the fact that, in some respects, I am becoming increasingly fond of the wild kids with their long hair, their unwashed bodies, their four-letter Anglo-Saxon words, and their raucous contempt for sacred cows. In a very straightforward and uncomplicated manner, I feel that they are probably the only truly religious people in our society. Whether consciously or unconsciously, they are protesting blasphemy.

This may come as something of a surprise to my friends, who know me as a very devout man. I accept literally the concept of the virgin birth, the trinity, and the resurrection. To me, these things happen and at a communion service I am literally drinking the blood and eating the body of Christ. I am merely bored with the earnest, emancipated, pedestrian minds who explain to me with such fervor that these concepts are superstitious hangovers from spring fertility rites, Babylonian mythology, and Greek philosophy. They tell me nothing that I do not know. I am aware of fertility rites, I have some idea of Babylonian mythology, and I have a deep respect for Greek philosophy, which spoke truths that have not been so well stated in over 2,000 years. All of this is totally irrelevant.

The basic point is that my unquestioning faith begins and ends at the communion rail. On all other matters, I reserve the right of skeptical judgment. And I believe that the only real blasphemy—the deadliest of sins—is the deification of mortals and the sanctification of human institutions. We are guilty of this sin and retribution is certain.

How many of us have sat without protest through meetings where glorified nonentities expounded profound platitudes in the awkward, ungainly language of modern liturgy—the "creative" nonthought and the "innovative" nonproposal? How many of us have writhed in secret agony while "dedicated" mediocrities have responded with the organization man's version of alleluia: "That grabs me. Run it up the flagpole and I'll salute it"?

These obscenities have become the condition of life in the modern world—in business, in labor, in liberal and conservative organizations, in publishing, in education, and even in our churches. And when they reach government, where decisions are life and death for hundreds of millions of people, they reach the ultimate of the intolerable. Under such circumstances the Four Horsemen ride not as a dreaded force but as a welcome relief.

Some of us should have stood up earlier and screamed some four-letter words. Really, nothing else was adequate as a protest to the occasion. We were restrained—not out of fear but out of our carefully cultivated reverence for institutions which were holy only in the sense that all men and women are children of God, which is quite a different thing from deification.

The kids, of course, are tragically wrong because they would destroy not only obscenity but the tradition of civility, which is probably the closest to excellence of any product of Western civilization. But their rage and their invective are wholly understandable. It fits far too much of the world in which we live. I do not like four-letter words and normally have reserved them for moments of great stress when they were essential to preserve sanity. But they describe the situation.

Things that are truly holy cannot be splattered no matter what is thrown at them. And that which can be befouled deserves its fate.

Somehow this thing must be made human again. Somehow we must learn to govern our people from an office that is secular and not from a court that is sanctified. If our destruction comes, it will be because we placed our faith—our unquestioning faith—in institutions that were only brick and wood and in men who were only flesh and blood and this seems to be the condition of the last half of the twentieth century.

★

Index

Adams, Sherman, 51, 53, 59
Army, 190, 191–92

Bailey, John, 66–67
Barkley, Alben W., 42
Bay of Pigs, see Cuba
Borah, William E., 80
Bridges, Styles, 52
Brown, H. Rap, 185
Bryan, William Jennings, 62

Cabinet, see Presidency, cabinet
Capote, Truman, 46
Carter, Clifton C., 67
Castro, Fidel, 34
Cleveland, Grover, 62
Clifford, Clark, 46
Communications, see Press; Television
Communism:
  as international plot, 176–77
  Truman charged as "soft" on, 14, 43
Congress:
  power of initiative limited, 39
  power delegated to, 5, 35, 37, 47
  and the president, 19–20, 31, 35, 37, 38–41, 80–81, 82–83, 127–30, 145, 146–47
  see also House of Representatives; Senate
Congressional Record, 79, 106
Connally, John, 141–42
Constitution:
  executive branch (presidency), 5–9, 34–35, 127
    disability provision, 170–71, 172–73
    terms limited, 58, 62, 139
  judicial branch, 5, 7, 37
  legislative branch, 5, 35, 37, 47
  power, checks and balances on, 5–6, 34, 36–37, 47
Constitutional convention, possible, 184
Coolidge, Calvin, 18, 150
Courts, see Judiciary
Cuba, 34
  Bay of Pigs, 12, 31–32, 115
  missile crisis, 73–74

Dawson, William L., 112, 113
Democratic party:
  left wing groups, 64, 125
  nomination (1948), 42, 126

nomination (1952), 150–52
nomination (1964), 65–66
nomination (1968), 59, 66–67, 69, 70, 71, 134
parties absorbed by, 123, 124
see also Political parties; individual candidates and presidents
Dewey, Thomas E., 62
Dominican Republic, 27–28, 39
Dulles, John Foster, 59
Duvalier, François, 34

Eisenhower, Dwight D.:
candidacy, 152
proposed by Democrats, 42
third term if allowed, 58, 62–63, 139
and Congress, 49–57, 82, 131
decision making and organizational methods, 30–31, 59
powers delegated, 21, 88, 140
disability after heart attack, 172
military - industrial complex warning, 19
popularity, 45–46, 49, 55, 57–58, 59–60, 71, 139–40
relaxation, 25
Russian satellite controversy, 49–54
staff, 85
television appearances, 161
Electoral College, 148, 153, 184

Farley, James, 150, 151
Fortas, Abe, 141

Gabriel Over the White House, 18
Garfield, James A., 155–56, 172
Goldwater, Barry, 65, 134

Haggerty, Jim, 21, 59, 88
Harding, Warren G., 18, 49, 149–150

Harriman, Averell, 150
Henry, Patrick, 6
Hopkins, Harry, 96
House, Colonel Edward M., 86
House of Representatives:
proposal to extend term, 137, 138, 145, 147
see also Congress
Humphrey, George, 51, 59
Humphrey, Hubert H., presidential campaign, 69, 70, 71, 132

Jackson, Andrew, 6, 8
Jefferson, Thomas, 144
Johnson, Lyndon B.:
airline strike (1966), 68, 94–95
cabinet, 74
campaign, 65, 66, 157–58
civil rights and welfare legislation, 19
Commerce and Labor departments, attempted merger, 13–14
and Congress, relations with as president, 82–83
decision making, 103–04
control over detail, 21
"credibility gap," 67–68, 95
Democratic party organization resented, 66–67
Dominican Republic, 27–28, 39
Fortas nomination as chief justice, 141
Negroes, problems of, 187–88
nuclear nonproliferation treaty, 140
and the press, 110
refusal to run again, 67, 68–69, 139, 140
relaxation, 26, 175
in Senate, 51–55, 57, 131
and Shivers, Allen, 141–42

Stevenson backed, 151
television appearances, 158, 161, 162, 163
Vietnam, 32, 39, 40, 68, 140
youth, dealings with, 188
Journalism, *see* Press
Judiciary:
disputes adjudicated, 5, 37
as agency for social change, 7
power of initiative limited, 39
and the president, 81

Kefauver, Estes, 150–51
Kennedy, John F.:
assassination, 139, 155
Bay of Pigs, 12, 31–32
cabinet as institution scorned by, 73, 74
and Congress, 41, 82
Cuban missile crisis, 73–74
equal - employment-opportunity commission set up, 41
New York Herald-Tribune canceled, 105
nomination and campaign, 57, 63, 66
relaxation, 26, 175
television appearances, 159, 161, 163
Kennedy, Robert F.:
assassination, 158
Cuban missile crisis, 73–74
presidential bid, 68, 69–70
Kerr, Robert S., 150
Knebel, Fletcher, *Night at Camp Camp David*, 170
Knox, Frank, 129
Korean War, 14, 27, 44, 150
Krim, Arthur, 46

Labor disputes, 94–95, 186
Legislature, *see* Congress; House of Representatives; Senate

Lincoln, Abraham, 6, 118, 144, 155, 156, 160

MacArthur, Douglas, Truman's removal of, 43, 44–45
McCarthy, Eugene, presidential bid, 67, 68, 69, 134
McKinley, William, 31, 156
McNamara, Robert S., 74
McPherson, Harry, 86
Marshall, John, 7
Montgomery, Robert, 161

Negroes:
Johnson's programs for, 187–88
as militants, 136, 187–89, 190–191, 192, 193
Neustadt, Richard E., 20, 136
Nixon, Richard M.:
antiballistic missile system, 83
cabinet, 130
campaign (1960), 62
campaign (1968), 62, 70–71, 132
and Congress, 83
income-tax surcharge, 83
nuclear nonproliferation treaty, 140–41
popularity, 189–90
relaxation, 26
staff, 90
television appearances, 161
Vietnam, 136–37, 190
youth, dealings with, 189
Nuclear nonproliferation treaty, 140–41

Orwell, George, 106, 110
Otis, James, 6

Paine, Thomas, 6
Parliamentary system:
parties, 152, 183

and presidency, 71–72, 178–79, 182–83
prime minister, 166, 178–79
question, 164–65
Police, 190–91
Political parties, 119–35
  bipartisanship, 127–28
  as coalitions (two-party systems), 123–27, 124, 152–53
  criticism of, 131–35, 152–53, 183
  conventions, 132–33
  "party responsibility," 122, 134–135
  platform, 125–26
  and the president, 119, 121–22
  see also Democratic party; Republican party
Politics:
  held in low esteem, 120
  leadership, 144, 189, 194
  power, nature of, 33–34, 84, 122, 138, 153
  and the press:
    "favorites," 115–16
    honesty in reporting, 114–15
    points of view contrasted, 100, 111–12
    possible regulation of, 113
  pressure groups, 142
  revolutionary elements, dealing with, 192
  see also Presidency, political ability
Power, separation of, 5–6, 34, 36–37, 47
Presidency:
  advisers, 10–14, 23–24
    government "experts," 143–44
    see also below staff
  cabinet, 73–79, 134
  and Congress, 31, 35, 37, 38–41,

80–81, 82–83, 130, 145, 146–147
  bipartisanship, 127–29
  as popularity wanes, 81, 130
  roles, difference in, 19–20
  credibility, importance of, 107–108
  decision making, 20–26, 28, 29, 30, 31–32
    psychological burdens it imposes, 21, 24, 81
    public support sought, 29, 57, 81–82, 83
    responsibilities, 32, 48–49
    see also below political ability; power and authority
  disability provision in Constitution, 170–71, 172–73
  and judiciary, 81
  mediocre and great presidents, 29
  opposition within government, lack of, 73–84
  and parliamentary system, 71–72, 178–79, 182–83
  personality traits:
    accentuated by office, 18
    importance of, 20
    irrationality and neurosis as result of office, 22–23, 169–170, 173–80
    office not stereotyped, 19–20
    privilege, effect of, 12, 15–16, 23–24, 80, 160
    sense of destiny and identification with history, 15, 18, 27, 28
    television exposure as damaging, 160–61, 163, 166
  political ability, 14–15, 20, 48–49, 139, 142, 144–45, 154
    during campaign, 61–62
    and party, 119, 121–22

as possible test of rationality, 177–78, 180
power and authority, 5–9, 34–35, 38–39, 47
  associates benefit, 46
  domestic affairs, 40–41
  foreign affairs and defense, 39, 40, 127
  initiative, 39–41
  see also above decision making
and the press, *see* Press privileges, 4–5, 8–10
  personality affected by, 12, 15–16, 23–24, 80, 160
and the public:
  accessibility, 156–59
  support for programs, 27, 57, 81–82, 83
reality, contact with, 96
  during campaigns, 157–59
  through press, *see above* press
reality, isolation from, 3, 8–9, 12, 23–24, 95, 97–98, 106, 137, 166–67, 193
reform, proposals for, 136–54
  "assistant presidents," 137
  national primaries, 148–53
  parliamentary system, 178–79, 182–83
  political pressure lessened, 137–38
  single term of six years, 137, 138–39, 142
and regulatory agencies, 81
staff, 9–10, 85–98
  access to president, importance of, 88–89, 92, 93
  image of president projected by, 169
  in-fighting, 90–91
  isolation of president from reality, 23–24, 97–98
offices, 89–90
personal secretary, 89
press office and press secretary, 21, 22, 86, 87–88
special assistant for national security affairs, 86–87
special counsel, 86
of "strong" vs. "weak" president, 98
wrong problems brought to attention, 94
television appearances, 41–42, 46, 102, 104, 116, 159–62, 166
press conferences, 162–65
terms, limitation on, 58, 62, 139
terms, myths of, 62–63
Presidential campaigns, 61–62
candidacy at wrong time, 61, 71
as means of contact with public, 157–59
on television, 159
Press:
and politics:
  "favorites," 115–16
  honesty in reporting, 114–15
  points of view contrasted, 100, 111–12
  possible regulation by, 113
and the president, 41–42, 46, 99–118
  "favorite" reporters, 102, 103, 109–10
  items "traded," 102, 112
  manipulation by, 100–01, 107, 110
  news conferences on television, 162–65
  press office and press secretary, 21, 22, 86, 87–88
"sources," 116

Rayburn, Sam, 57, 150, 151

Reagan, Ronald, 70, 193
Republican party:
    nomination (1912), 126
    nomination (1920), 149–50
    nomination (1964), 63–65, 134
    nomination (1968), 70–71
    right wing groups, 64–65, 125
    see also Political parties; indi-
        vidual candidates and pres-
        idents
Revolutionary   movements   in
    America, 187–94
Rockefeller, Nelson, 70
Romney, George, 70
Roosevelt, Franklin D., 6, 144, 160
    Axis, decision to resist, 27
    bipartisanship, 129
    and Congress, 82
    "Fala" speech, 30
    political ability, 30, 46–47, 49,
        95–96, 108–09
    popularity, 71
        attacks on, 58, 59, 118, 169–
        170
    presidential terms limited be-
        cause of him, 62, 139
    "quarantine the aggressors," 30
    relaxation, 25
    staff, 86, 95–96
    Supreme Court "packing," 14,
        47
Roosevelt, Mrs. Franklin D., 54
Roosevelt, Theodore, 6, 38, 103
Rosenman, Samuel, 109
Rossiter, Clinton, 136
Rusk, Dean, 74
Russell, Richard B., 45, 150–51

Sandburg, Carl, 156
Secret Service, 10, 157
Senate:
    political realism, 79–80, 84

    and the president, 80–81
    see also Congress
Shivers, Allen, 141–42
Sorensen, Theodore, 86
Soviet Union, 34, 50–51, 140
    see also Communism
Stevenson, Adlai, 66, 111, 152
    presidential campaign, 150, 151,
        152
Stimson, Henry L., 129
Students, 136, 187–88, 189, 190–91,
    192, 193
Supreme Court, *see* Judiciary

Television, and the president, 41–
    42, 46, 102, 104, 116, 159–
    166
Teller, Edward, 52–53
Truman, Harry S, 5, 18, 19
    campaign and election, 42–43
    and Congress, 82, 130–31, 147
    Communism, charged as being
        "soft" on, 14, 43
    Korean War, 14, 27, 44, 150
    language criticized, 175
    MacArthur, removal of, 43, 44–
        45
    political ability, 42–44
    on president as final authority,
        24
    press biased against, 118
    refusal to run again, 139
    relaxation, 25–26
    scandals in administration, 150
    on Secret Service, 157
    steel mill seizure, 6
    and Wallace, Henry, 76

Udall, Stewart L., 74

Vietnam, 11, 39, 40, 192
    Johnson, 32, 39, 40, 68, 140

Nixon, 136–37, 190
opposition to, 136, 187, 191
Violence, means of dealing with,
 185–87, 188–91

Wallace, George:
presidential bid, 71, 132
as type, 193

Wallace, Henry A., 76–77
Weisl, Edwin L., 52
White, William S., 109–10
Wilson, Charles, 59
Wilson, Woodrow:
disability after stroke, 172
Germany, ultimatum to, 31
House as adviser, 86
League of Nations, 14, 146–47

About the Author

George E. Reedy served in the Johnson Administration as Special Assistant to the President. He was also a member of the President's National Advisory Commission on Selective Service. Mr. Reedy's distinguished career has also included the following positions: Press Secretary to President Johnson; Executive Director of the Senate Democratic Policy Committee (1953–1960); Senate correspondent for the United Press (1949–1951); United Press correspondent for the House of Representatives (1946–1949). He has also served on mediation boards in the settlement of various labor-management disputes. At present Mr. Reedy is a lecturer and consultant on labor-management relations, oceanography, and public affairs. He is the author of *Who Will Do Our Fighting for Us?*